WALK WITH ME

It's Not About Getting It Right

JESSIE DECORSEY

WALK
WITH
ME

Unless otherwise marked, scripture quotations are taken from the *Holy Bible*, New
Living Translation, copyright ©1996, 2004, 2015 by Tyndale House Foundation. Used
by permission of Tyndale House Publishers, Carol Stream, Illinois 60188. All rights
reserved.

ISBN: 979-8-9896215-0-7

Library of Congress Control Number: 2023923465

Cover Art by Jessie DeCorsey
Printed by Ingram Spark
First paperback edition 2024
www.jessiedecorsey.com

To my husband, Trevor

Your love changes the world. Thank you for always believing in me and walking with me through this life.

CONTENTS

INTRODUCTION
TREVOR DECORSEY

The door swung open in our split level entryway and a young lady bounced up the stairs. Her shiny brown hair had touches of blonde wound into her perfect spiral curls. Her cheeks shimmered ever so slightly as the light hit the makeup on her face. There was a sparkle in her eyes and a joyful glow radiating from her smiling face as my sister introduced her to our family. I was seventeen and in my final year of high school. Little did I know that I was meeting my future wife for the first time that day.

This memory always makes me smile. I don't typically remember these sorts of things when meeting people. This image has played back in my mind many times and it's one I won't soon forget. Jessie was pretty and charismatic but she was my sister's friend so I had planned to leave it that way. It's just an unspoken rule at that age, but sometimes rules are more of guidelines I guess. Over time I had a change of mind and a change of plans.

The next year we began to hang out more and more. We grew closer as we got to know each other, and I was surprised to learn how different our family life and upbringing was. My parents were married and we all lived in the same home. Jessie's parents had divorced when she was a young child and she lived with her mom while her brother lived with her father who I'd never met. I couldn't wrap my head around the fact that her brother and her didn't live together. The more I learned about all she had been through growing up, the more my heart ached. It ached at the pain she had already been through and the pain that would come to pass that I could do nothing about. I didn't understand much of what I had walked into or how this could actually be her everyday 'normal'. I couldn't help but wonder how she wasn't more broken. She had some deep wounds yet she still had that joyful glow. She was absolutely beautiful. So was her heart.

Growing up I never really had big over the top dreams. I didn't have any desire to be famous or well known. I never imagined myself with a big fancy career and a big salary. Sometimes it was hard enough to figure out how I was going to financially be able to move out of my parent's house at that age. What I did know I wanted for my life was a wife and a family of my own.

Sometimes that's all I can remember thinking about my future. Trying to imagine what it would look like and what kind of husband or father I would be. What would my wife be like? Getting married at a young age was actually the beginning of my dream come true. At that time we had more than enough criticism and people sharing their opinion on how we were too young. They shared their doubts but didn't seem to have the time to get to know us to understand how we felt about each other.

We didn't care what they thought. At least I didn't. We married with little more than the love we shared.

On these pages I read such an honest and vulnerable testimony of our story and it brought me back to all the heartache of that time. Remembering how I used to wonder if my love was going to be enough for Jessie. As my feelings began to surface, I had tears running down my cheeks. These tears contained some healing within them. Reading her words now as she was recognizing how much I had loved her in all those past challenging moments, really hit me. The tears continued as I was realizing that it all mattered back then. It had made a difference. She was answering questions I'd only thought to myself from a long time ago. This felt like the healing I had once hoped for but had long since forgotten about.

God hadn't forgotten. God knew the desires of my heart, the real meaningful desires and He has given me mine. Jessie and our children were answers to the prayers I didn't even realize I had prayed for. I believe that all those times I would think about my future and what I wanted for my life had been prayers. God also knows when our hearts have hurt inside and He doesn't forget that either. He knew my heart needed some healing and the way I received it today was through my wife's story.

Through her journey and the way she has written out these parts of our life so tenderly and gently, allowed the bruises from my past to heal. Her words found me in the autumn woods of Minnesota during the deer hunting season. This is my favorite place to be and my favorite time of year. There's an hour during the sunrise or sunset where the light illuminates the woods in such a magnificent way it brings with it awe and wonder. I love to marvel at every shade of red, orange and yellow leaves that we see in our hills and river valleys during this season and although the trees are nearly bare and the color has faded away, I still love being submersed in the woods. I feel so at peace and find it to be a place I can connect with God through nature. I can see in my mind why I am out here as I'm reading through these emotional parts of our story.

And in this story is a reminder that it's not about getting things right and never has been. What is right anyway? Who would be the authority to declare what we choose is right? Wouldn't that depend vastly on the circumstances we find ourselves in? The experiences we've had in our own lives? There are so many factors to consider and it might be different for everyone. Just trying to declare what is right might actually be something we get wrong. Think about that for a moment. That's a mind bending thought for me. It's not about whether we get things right but rather it's about how we can walk through this life with Him in a relationship. That's all He's ever wanted. With Him we will find more love, grace (especially for ourselves) and more of the peace He wants for us. With Him we will have far more opportunities to receive the healing He is trying to bring to us that we sometimes bury and forget we need like what I've found in and through this book. We will be able to receive and share the love He has freely given us. Life is better when we walk with Him without the fear of getting things wrong. As Jessie and I have come to learn through our life together which she so graciously shares through her revelations and how that came about in this book.

When I read this, "Life can only be understood backwards, but it must be lived forwards," I stopped to think about how it is only when we look back that we can see the bigger picture or have a better understanding of where God was in our life. Reading these pages helped me realize that when we went through some of our challenges, I could see how they shaped me into the man I am today. I could see how we had both been shaped and those challenges become the areas of strength we each carry now. As you read this, I believe it may help you see where God was at certain times in your life that you couldn't see in the moment.

My wife's story has been a beautiful thing that gives me a feeling of joy and excitement when I think about it. We are both finding healing and walking together as we do. I was made to love Jessie with everything I have. I've found it an easy thing to do because I know who she is and I know the love and goodness she carries in her heart. I've also found that once in a while love has to endure some pain so that its real value can be known. And in walking with Him the healing will come.

1

TWO LOST GIRLS

I was recently sitting with a friend who I've been journeying with for a short time and getting to know. We have been connecting to pray and work out some of the difficult chapters of our lives and share our stories. In our last meeting Jesus spoke these words to her, "It's not about getting it right, it's about walking it out with me."

You know those moments when something is spoken to someone else, but the words connect to your soul. They permeate your spirit and land in such a way that you carry them with you – like a new extension of yourself. A truth or understanding that brings light into a place that was void and dark. This was a moment where God lit a torch for me and I started to examine the words He spoke to us that day in lieu of the journey towards healing I had been on.

The last five years I've been committed to deep diving into my past and resolving areas of my life that seem to be stuck. One thing I have learned is that striving, for me, is something that seems to be persistently unresolvable. Time and time again something will rise to the surface in my life that I am pursuing with a striving heart. Even the words, "It's not about getting it right," offend me in a way. Aren't our social constructs and religions based on this notion of getting things right? I've never been one to be okay with getting things wrong. That seems to lead to a consequence of some kind – I tend to avoid the pain of getting things wrong as often as I can. In fact, I avoid pain to such a degree I will do almost anything to escape it.

To strive refers to one who is fighting, contending, or straining to achieve something or working hard. The opposite of striving would be relaxing, resting, yielding or surrendering. Striving for me became a tool to keep myself from hurting, even though the reality was that striving was the very thing keeping me from healing. "My identity is ultimately shaped by who I love and what pain I avoid. Love and the pain I avoid often compete within me to see whether my love or my fear of pain is stronger."[1]

Much of my identity was driven by the pain I was avoiding because that seemed to be safest. In relationships or situations, my focus would tend to be on the person or thing that had the potential to be the most dangerous. I would problem solve what I would have to do to neutralize my environment constantly. The root of this was unresolved pain, which without realizing it, became the driving force of my perfectionism, people pleasing and a distorted relationship with God. Striving and working in my own strength often gave me control over my circumstances

16

and allowed me to not depend on others. People can't hurt you if you don't let them help you. This seemed to work well for a time but eventually the foundation I had built my life on to keep myself from feeling pain came crashing down. And with it the false identity I had been accustomed to. On the outside I looked whole but on the inside I was fractured and imprisoned.

I was born into a broken home where chaos and dysfunction were the foundation of my youth. To combat the level of constant change and loneliness, I became addicted to performance and achievement. Being academically inclined I was happy to give myself away to my studies, filling the unhappiness and voids with self-motivational speeches on how to be an honor roll student. Having control and being self-sufficient also became a way in which I found I could create my own happy oasis in what was otherwise a rather detached deserted adolescence.

I grew up with a single mother, just the two of us for the most part. My brother who is 5 years older than me lived with our dad cities away. Mom was a brilliant artist and entrepreneur and a model for creativity and hard work. Despite the many hardships she faced in her life, she never showed any signs of weakness or gave any setbacks much time. To this day she is the strongest person I know.

We didn't talk about God in our home. With occasional visits to my grandma's church on Easter, I remember little outside of the dresses my mother would buy me to wear. My parents divorced when I was four years old and I don't have a single memory of the two of them together in a home. Any interaction between them was fighting over custody and child support.

My father at one time was an evangelist with a burning desire to share the gospel, but somewhere along the way he fell far from the church and people. I would see my dad occasionally with split custody and remember a few conversations about Jesus and some powerful testimonies, but I was never able to reconcile much about my heavenly dad. Even still, there was a seed planted in my young self that believed in the God of my father. I remember being a fervent prayer at the age of five. I prayed for healing over my parents because I wanted my family back together. I can still remember almost every word of those prayers as if they are still echoing into eternity. Every night I would recite the same words over and over again. I don't remember how old I was when I gave up. But I do know that was when I stopped believing that prayer really mattered to God. Or that I mattered much to God. That little girl crying out for a father to come back home had to find a way to cope with heartache too painful and too complex to reconcile. Unbeknownst to me, this trauma would govern my heart and all the relationships to come.

There was always something I felt separated me from the rest of the kids at school who had families and spent time together. I noticed most of them attended church and I suppose a part of me hungered for both as they seemed to go hand and hand for everyone else. In our small town in rural Minnesota I only knew of two churches, and as far as I was concerned the entire world consisted only of Catholics and Lutherans. I have a vivid memory of a conversation between a family member and myself around the age of ten. The word had gotten to this person that I wasn't baptized as an infant. They told me that I was going to hell if I didn't do this. I was terrified. I thought I was saved when I was little, my dad had said all I had to do was ask Jesus into my heart. So I did that every night just to be sure He was in there. The thought of being unsaved became something of a death sentence that attached itself into my youngest understanding of God and a father's love.

At some point in my young teens, depression and self-hate crept masterfully into my poorly formed identity. Bullied at school for being overweight and mocked because of my off-brand wardrobe I lost any sense of compassion towards myself. The world informed my identity. The world was cruel. I found other things like substance abuse to pacify the loneliness and unworthiness I felt in school. Drinking on my way to student council meetings before school started in the 7th grade. My mom was unaware because of my continued report card achievements. I suppose her lack of noticing my need for help became an internal motivator for finding approval in all the wrong places. Something we talk openly about now. She recently said, "At one point you pushed me away and I let you. Looking back now, I know I shouldn't have done that." I remember those moments. When I would test and close the door to her attempts to connect. The door would stay closed. She gave me what she believed I wanted. As a mother to a 13 year old myself, I can understand this age and appreciate the independence that comes along with it. How was she to know the wounding message that would wire in me was that I was unwanted and unlovable? The very last thing in the world she wanted me to feel.

Mom was a contender for finding love, only she found a world of betrayal and always married the same kind of wrong. I watched her get hurt time and time again and rebuild our life from the ground up. Despite how lonely we both were we managed to get by and laugh at one another on occasion. My mother had a beautiful way of not taking herself too seriously and her perseverance is something I admire in her to this day. There was still something special to the friendship we developed in those years despite the silence between the walls – the two lost girls.

2
STARS OF PROMISE

Because our lives at the time were in constant transition and I found myself alone more often than not, I was struggling to find my worth. People pleasing became a strategy I found the most safety in. During middle school, I started attaching my identity and value to others opinions of me. Finding ways to become as likeable and pleasing to my peers to gain their favor often led me to unhealthy relationships, unsafe situations and experiences well beyond my years and maturity. I had no real sense of belonging to a people outside of my classmates. I would do almost anything to win their approval and avoid the faces of rejection. Since our identity is the one thing our brain cannot create on its own it relies heavily on our experiences, our memories and the faces that love us to tell us who we are. Dr. Jim Wilder, author and neurotheologian explains, "Our identity really is, what I have seen mirrored to me, is who I know myself to be."[1] Looking back, I can see how desperate I was to experience some reflection of value in the faces of the people I loved. It seemed to only come if I was behaving in a way that pleased them.

Several of my friends at the time invited me to their youth group meetings at church. Up until this time I had been carrying a deep unreconciled belief that I was going to hell and was very keen on asking the pastor of the church to baptize me which he happily obliged. I remember those Wednesday nights, starting to come alive in the possibilities of Jesus. A heavenly Father who loved me. I still didn't really understand what He had to do with God or how they had anything to do with each other. I was happy to combine them into one concept and call it good. Call it God. I remember sharing with my youth group a few times where something supernatural had happened and I knew God was speaking to me through it. I distinctly remember my youth leader's eyes getting big and her delight in hearing my stories.

The first dream I remember seeing or hearing God happened when I was 12. I had been praying every night repenting for being sinful and I didn't want to be anymore. In the dream I was floating in Lake Superior, a large body of crystal clear water we have here in Minnesota. I was repenting and suddenly I heard God speak through the clouds above me telling me I was clean and there were no stains of sin on me. At that age I still hadn't been able to comprehend what Christ had done for me. But in that moment, encountering God in my dream, I knew that I was forgiven. I stopped repenting after that for being a sinner. Looking back that dream marked a moment of freedom from a faulty belief system. That dream was the beginning of my restoration story – finding my true identity.

These were the kind of stories I would share with anyone who would lend an ear at church. The pastor at Trinity Lutheran took me under his wing and invited me to come to the church once a week so I could catch up for the years of youth group I had missed. I wanted to get confirmed with my classmates because that seemed to be the thing that a Christian should do. I would walk into his office where he sat with a warm presence and a kind smile. In his tender voice he would lecture me on scripture and things I ought to know about the life of Jesus. I had to memorize the Ten Commandments and the Lord's Prayer and he would laugh at me and seemed rather amused at my eagerness to learn. He said, "You come here every week and sit with me and I believe you are actually paying attention to what I'm saying and not just nodding your head." He was right. I was fascinated with the things he was saying. It was all new to me and there was a sense of self growing and new life. His kindness has stayed with me all these years. The time he sat with me and the way he made me feel seen was a great gift to a lost girl.

The Lord often brings me back to those memories when Him and I come together these days. He shows me how present He was in orchestrating moments like sitting in a pastors office memorizing scripture. Those days when I often found myself alone, I would go outside and lay under the star lit sky. It was the first time I started to understand the majesty and glory of God. Right there on display in the stars. I would recall the Lord's Prayer and Nicene Creed and as I did I grew more and more aware of the one I was connecting to. The idea of God started becoming a relationship with God motivating a change in my heart. Almost overnight I walked away from people and paths of destruction I had been on. Even destructive things I was doing to myself. The dysfunction and abusive patterns I was using to fill a void no longer felt like home. I was finding a new home in my creator. I was finding Him.

A few years ago I found an old journal from those stargazing days in my attic as I was looking for something in a box of old memories. Inside were the faces of my best friends from school and cuttings from popular teen magazines. My heart broke for the emotions that younger me was expressing through the artwork inside. I hadn't remembered until I saw the words; *HELP, Pressure, A+, The Faces of Depression* and a cut out of Steve Urkel glued to the cover. The feelings flooded back as I turned the page and saw my Dad's pager number written down. It was probably the most I had of him at the time. The next pages revealed a pleasant surprise. Taped securely to the notepad were the very clippings of the Lord's Prayer I had gotten from the church with a journal entry that read;

November 19, 1998

I never used to know this prayer because I never went to church. But when I started going every time everyone would say this prayer. But last Sunday I went and I cut this out of a flyer that I found. Now I feel a little better because all I need to do is look in this and there it is. OR maybe if I read it long enough I'll memorize it. I feel a lot better now that I go to confirmation.

Turning the yellowed pages that were stained by time revealed more of my story.

The Earth is filled with your light and goodness, evidence of your gracious love for us. We dedicate these promises of time, talent, energy and money as symbols of the giving of ourselves. Fill us with new joy to serve you, that the brightness of your generous care may spread to all, until the day it shines in full, through Christ our light amen.

Be with us now and bless us as we dedicate these gifts to your glory and praise. Grant us joy in them and lead us to the building up of your kingdoms.

November 25th, 1998
All these clippings that I clip out are from Sunday church. I'm not sure why I clip these all out, maybe its cause I feel holeyer (sp?) or something. Cause then all I do is read them and it's just like I'm praying.

25

November 25th, 1998 – Second Entry
Here is all of my opinions about love. No matter how
much you say you love a person or how much you write
it, it will never be true unless you feel it...

This new language that I didn't fully understand started to transform my thinking and my inner turmoil. I wanted to feel love and I was longing to be seen and known. As I read the next few entries of my old journal I wept in that dark dust filled attic.

December 13th, 1998
Stars are more than stars to me its heaven....I don't
know if stars mean that to anyone else...

I continued talking about my friend at the time who also loved stars and how much we had in common. Both of us felt depressed and wanted more out of our lives than drugs and who we were becoming. We were in a circle of friends who found connection being lost kids. Initially they welcomed me and admired the fact that I wouldn't touch a cigarette. Eventually the safety and love I felt from them led me to partake in whatever they were doing. Before I knew it, smoking weed and drinking became a natural part of my day to day. Beneath the surface I didn't like how it made me feel and what it was doing to me. But I didn't know how to move away from it or move away from the people who I had come to know and love. Looking back I can see how God met me in the place of not knowing what to do and created a new path. I was crying out for help and He answered me. This journal was a time capsule of memories. Everything I had suppressed and buried over the years and completely forgotten. It seemed that this was a key to understanding some of the reasons I was finding myself stuck today. So often we want memories to stay in the past but when they are unresolved or unhealed they live in our present. This was a rescue mission to descend to the darkest cavern of my youth and rescue the lost girl within by remembering her story.

December 13th, 1998

Picture yourself blind, never seeing anything in your life. The way I would describe it would be blackness. Nothingness, sometimes evilness. I know that I couldn't think. All my thoughts would be jumbled and senseless....and sometimes I would sit there and in my head be screaming and screaming for my mom to come stop me. To find out where I really was and what I was doing.

At the age of 14, I had found myself attached to unhealthy behaviors trying to avoid the pain of loneliness. I didn't have words to convey or the ability to understand, to know that what I was missing was attunement and love. I *knew* I was loved but the pain of loneliness was more present in our home and spoke louder to me. My mother worked hard those days to keep a roof over our head and we scarcely crossed paths. I had little to no relationship with my brother or father. I thought if I worked hard enough and did everything perfect that would make me worthy of love. It was all coming back to me. I marveled as I read the words I used to express the emptiness I was feeling and the spiritual darkness I was surrounded in – looking for light. Looking for the One who is love and His kingdom of which I knew little of.

In his book, *The Power to Bless*, Alan Wright shares "Without capacity for language, we are less than human."[2] He illustrates this powerfully with a quote from Hellen Keller who didn't experience real humanity until she discovered speech.

> For nearly six years I had no concept of nature or mind or death or God, I literally thought with my body…then suddenly…I awoke to language, to knowledge of love, to the visual concepts of nature, of good and evil! I was actually lifted from nothingness to human life.[3]

In that season of church nights, Sunday mornings, a gentle pastor who spoke life over me, the baptismal waters and the awakened sense of nature and God in creation over my head in the night sky, I started to learn a new language. A language of love. It was more than a word, it was a feeling. It was an experience rooted deep within my healing heart. Something that whispered that I was made for more in this lifetime. Something more than what I was experiencing in the loneliness of a broken home or a substance. I started to shift away from nothingness.

I recall my last binge and the end of darkness. It felt like a battle over my identity because something was trying to keep me in a state of confusion. I distinctly remember a loud antagonizing thought come into my mind that started mocking the existence of God. A screaming voice that tried to come against this new love I had discovered in Christ. Is God even real? Is any of it real? I distinctly remember turning away from that lifestyle from that moment on. I wasn't about to exchange this new feeling for one that beckoned me back to nothingness. Not anymore. There were too many stars in the sky and each one sang a song of promise.

October 21st, 1999
You can change your mind but your heart and soul must be willing.

These last words written in the journal were crammed on the bottom of the page after I mentioned a valuable lesson I learned through the process of transformation. I was now a freshman in high school and boasting of my grades and how I was finding myself. I listed several crushes and my deep desire to live life to the fullest and seize every moment to experience joy. The words inked on the pages spoke into my desire to break away from all the negative things in my life that were keeping me down. One of my friends during this time had gotten into treatment and came back a different person. I had noted how proud I was and how quickly a person can change if they are willing. I realized that change required willingness and it needed to come from the heart, not the head. No one can make that choice for us but they can give us an invitation.

I no longer attended church because confirmation ended but I was still experiencing God around me in creation. I continued to focus on school with a deep love of the arts which I inherited from my mother who now owned and operated a framing studio and art gallery in our small town. Leaving destructive relationships in her past – it seemed we were both on a new path. We were ready for change.

In no time I was working several jobs, enrolled in community college while still in high school and falling in love with my now husband. These were the years I found myself in the arms of someone who I had determined God had created just for me, Trevor DeCorsey. He had already graduated high school when we started dating while I was a sophomore. I remember meeting his family for the first time. They were one of those families I had deemed perfect. They had a beautiful home full of love. They went to the Catholic Church every Sunday and had meals together. His mother was the most encouraging person I had ever met and they welcomed me into their home as if I was one of their own. In those years I was both thankful but also burdened by the truth of what home was supposed to feel like. The presence of Trevor's family made the absence of mine come to the surface in new ways. It made me fully aware of the things I had never gotten to experience which created other unhealthy ways of coping.

Trevor, my patient hero, showed me the love of the Father by picking up the pieces when I would fall apart day after day. When the voice of rejection would tell me I was unlovable and not enough, he was there to remind me that I was. He walked through the valley with me as I had developed an eating disorder and routinely pushed him away because his love for me at times was too real for an immature teen. I didn't know how to love him back the same. Not in the sacrificial way he loved me. But no matter how much I hurt him and hurt myself his love never wavered. He endured patiently, waiting for me to come back to him. He embodied the love of Christ to me. Never rejecting or condemning me – just waiting and loving me back to life. Once again God provided me with a new language of love, grace.

3

THE NARROW ROAD

"You can enter God's Kingdom only through the narrow gate. The highway to hell is broad, and its gate is wide for the many who choose that way. But the gateway to life is very narrow and the road is difficult, and only a few ever find it."

-Matthew 7:13-14

Matthew 7:13-14 was the only Bible verse I had ever memorized. I have no idea how old I was when it permeated my heart but it was the only one my Dad had ever spoken to me and I clung to it. I suppose the striver within wanted to always make sure I was on the narrow way and not the broad one. I had been on a path of destruction and I didn't want to go back. It didn't mean I didn't wander off every so often but the striver was always propelling me to work harder and to keep my eye focused on the narrow gate. Only I thought that was a call to performance and not a relationship. I was working towards perfectionism and success. I didn't know that entering the gate wasn't based on our works. The gate is Him. "Yes, I am the gate. Those who come in through me will be saved. They will come and go freely and will find good pastures."(John 10:9)

I started my counseling journey in my 30's because of a season of overwhelm I didn't know how to process alone. After a few months of counseling I was asked if I had ever experienced any childhood trauma. "No," I quickly replied. "Nothing traumatic." She then suggested that I go home and ask Trevor if he thought I had any childhood trauma. She explained that sometimes our loved ones can see things more easily about our lives than we can see for ourselves. I thought that sounded interesting but didn't expect him to respond any different than myself. As soon as I got home and started telling him about my session as I usually did, I decided to follow her advice. I asked him if he could see any trauma in my childhood. I remember his response vividly because it caught me off guard. "Jess you have so much trauma in your past – the craziest part of it is that you don't remember." He was right.

He started explaining things from the way he remembered – the countless times he would come to be with me because I was alone. The endless hours he would spend comforting the rejection I was feeling or the tears that he caught as I watched the hardships both of my parents were facing. The weekends I was alone as my mother found another companion to spend time with now that I was working and scarcely around myself. The façade I carried at the time to try to make myself look happy and beautiful on the outside when torrents of self-loathing accompanied me most of my time alone. Always lingering in my peripheral vision – always present as I fixed my gaze on working hard and people pleasing. Becoming what I thought the world wanted me to be. It's no wonder why I let the painful things get buried deep inside and internalized. I had a hope and a future and I was going to make it for myself and no one was going to stop me.

My last year of high school, I found myself immersed in studies of ancient mythologies that peaked my curiosities in world religions. I was enrolled almost entirely in college courses my senior year driving my rusty beat up truck back and forth to campus. I took in as many art courses as I could and the professor took a special liking to me, despite my young age, and let me co-lead her classes on occasion. She spoke a tremendous amount of identity into me as an artist. And with this new found confidence I wanted to study art and art history at university. Upon making this decision my mother warned me of choosing this path, pleading for me to pursue a degree in business or something else of that nature. She had been able to find stability as an artist herself by framing and selling art. She knew firsthand how hard it would be for me.

I couldn't argue her. I had grown up watching her work tirelessly to make ends meet, struggling to sell her own art. I had a high school teacher at the time that was encouraging me to consider a degree in art education. He loved his job as an art instructor and thought it was something I would like as well. Fear of failure made the decision for me. I didn't want to risk having an unsuccessful career as an artist but I also didn't want to let go of this part of my life. Becoming an art teacher made sense. I always identified as an artist. As young as the age of five I had people wanting to buy my drawings. It was something I always seemed to have a knack for and it was the one thing everyone seemed to champion about me. Being an artist was a place of refuge and safety that I could retreat to. A place that felt secure and untainted.

In June of 2003 I graduated high school and Trevor proposed to me. I couldn't wait to take his last name. Something inside of me wanted to sever all ties to my story of origin and have a new name. We went off to college together and were married a year later one hot July day in 2004. We had little to nothing to our name as we started building our life together, but I was used to this kind of building.

I was not a great wife in those early years. We were busy cramming for exams and working random jobs with little time in between for much else. Trevor was eager to start a family and I had no intentions of settling down whatsoever. The thought of a family had never really crossed my mind. We never spoke about our faith much and didn't attend a church. I was fighting a deep desire to have total freedom and to experience all the pleasure that this world had to offer which resulted in endless weekend binges and bars.

Being the only married couple on campus was challenging. The honeymoon days quickly wore off as fellow students and new acquaintances responded negatively asking why we rushed into marriage. I felt judged and insecure. My resolution was to live like a single and do whatever I wanted to do with little thought of how it was impacting Trevor. What I love about him to this day is that he still claims that loving me has been easy. HA! I remember one time living in a rental house in Northern Minnesota when he started to cry. This was something I hadn't seen before no matter what circumstances he had faced. He said, "I feel like I am losing you." And the ugly truth, he was losing me.

It's not easy to love someone who lives their life lost. Taking on a new name didn't resolve everything that I had hoped it would as a new identity. On occasion I would think about God but He had become something of the past. I was on my own path and I wasn't going to let anyone get in my way of where I wanted to go and what I wanted to accomplish in my life. However, that day when Trevor opened up his heart to me, there was a still small voice that pierced through the walls I had built up. I can picture the entire scene and the cry of my young faithful husband's heart. Here I was, on a destructive path, hurting the person I loved most. And once again I was faced with the choice to turn away from a lifestyle that had cunningly led me astray. The greatest gift in that process was growing a deeper love for Trevor and for our future together. I wanted him and I wanted to become the wife and partner he deserved. This opened me up to a moment of total surrender that marked a dramatic change in my relationship with God.

Also, during that time, we had a pair of cocker spaniels that had a litter of puppies. When they were born I had a favorite one that took after its dad and his markings. Within a week or so it became the runt and stopped eating altogether. To keep it alive I had to feed it every few hours day and night to make sure it would survive. One night I was inserting its feeding tube and it took its final breath in my hands and passed away. I had grown so attached to this little one it destroyed me. I couldn't understand what I had done wrong or what I could have done differently and it made me feel so powerless. I had no power over death. I had done everything I could do but it didn't matter because it was out of my control. Something in my spirit realized the fragility of creation and how every breath answers to the author of life in the end. My soul responded by lifting my eyes to Him and there I discovered a deep desire to give Jesus my life and everything I put my hands to, as I realized my life had been in his hands all along. I was starting to understand the gateway to life was trusting Him.

4
EPIPHANY

For as long as I can remember I wanted to travel the world. My junior year of college I got the opportunity to study abroad over J-term and dive into art and ancient civilizations in Greece. As I found myself walking the ancient ruins and getting lost in the study of mythology and the pantheon of gods, something unexpected happened. On the streets all around me were displays of Christianity erupting in ways I had never experienced before. The Greek Orthodox Church was alive and its heartbeat resounded through the atmosphere in contrast to the lifeless remnants of a lost religion under our feet. I can still smell the incense and feel the energy of thousands of people parading the streets in celebration of the Epiphany ceremony or the baptism of Christ and the blessing of the waters. Bishops adorned in priestly garments with icons parading down to the water's edge. A selected group of enthusiastic men from surrounding churches dove into the sea after a cross that was launched into its depths. A dramatic scene I still treasure as the victorious emerged from the water causing frenzy and a blessing atop his head. He was hoisted as a hero into the air and onto the shoulders of the swarming crowd.

There was something of the manifestation of God for me that day which felt like a new encounter. Religion up until then was quiet. In my life, no one but my father spoke about having dreams of God or moments when they felt or heard God speak to them. A relationship with God was only done corporately inside a building and it was never talked about. But here I witnessed freedom and celebration of faith. It had a sound and a voice and for the first time in my life I wanted to publically partake in a movement of the Spirit as people came together to joyfully express their love for Christ. In addition to that, the backdrop to the Greek Orthodox Church was their art and elaborate icons. There was something birthed in me during this experience that changed the way I wanted to express my faith through the things I was creating. I realized on that trip the magnitude of what people could create and the power of art to transcend reality as an agency of worship. I was profoundly moved by the iconography and the stories it told.

I came back from Greece with a new lens in which I saw the world and my place in it. I quickly changed my degree from art education to fine arts and art history. I started devouring books on Christianity to try to understand what it was I had experienced because I didn't want to let it go now that I returned home. I felt like a foreigner in my own land because I didn't see the movement of God around me anymore. I started using my art to understand who God was and who I was to God. I found a deep love and appreciation for Catholicism and spent a great deal researching the art of iconography. I had an instructor that partnered with me to dive into the Byzantium era and soon incorporated the colors and symbols into my own paintings. What really spoke to me during this time was reading the lives of the saints. They were ordinary people – not unlike myself. They had a deep hunger for Christ and experienced miraculous things as they listened for Him and followed His voice.

As I started painting a series of saints, I was really studying their stories and my hunger grew to know more about God's story. I was starting to see a new purpose and felt a deep calling to tell the stories of Christ in a modern context to see how it related to me – here and now. Up until this moment I had always felt removed from religion. What would it look like to have these stories personified today? How much more could we see ourselves in the stories of the Bible if they were more relatable? Would that inspire us to walk more freely and more fully outside of the walls of the church? These were the questions I started asking and I loved having this conversation with people as I exhibited my work. I started hearing how others, some for the first time, could see themselves differently. See God differently through the things I was creating.

Blending the ancient art form of Iconography with modern people did cause some push back. Some fellow students and professors didn't understand how my paintings would work for anything outside of a church and I was told they had no future audience. I wish I could tell you I let those comments slide right off of me but I believed they were true. I struggled through so much rejection from the art world during that time at university I wanted to quit. At one point I reached out to my professor from the community college I attended in high school to tell her how dejected I was feeling. She encouraged me to stay with it and push through. It turned out that part of why my Mother had encouraged me to stay away from studying art was because of the trials she faced as well. She quit after her first year of being enrolled in the same program at the same university as me. She understood exactly what I was going through and empathized. There is so much criticism when it comes to the arts. It has always been hard for me to understand why we focus so much on the critiquing of one another over championing the person and the expression they are sharing through their work.

After my senior exhibition and finishing university I started applying for graduate school to continue to explore different ways of creating meaningful artwork. I was dead set on moving to New York or Chicago to pursue higher level training. Meanwhile, Trevor supported my dreams and encouraged me in everything I did. Despite the fact that he was ready to settle down and plant roots somewhere, he was willing to go wherever I wanted. If he wanted a different life for us in this season I didn't have ears to hear it or eyes to see it. I was laser focused on becoming successful. Other students I was graduating with in the art program received full ride scholarships for their continued education. I was determined that I could qualify for one as well, without it there would be no affording it, so I knew I had to work harder than anyone else. I spent two years applying to programs all over the United States with Trevor resiliently by my side. I was working full-time at a Starbucks with an addition of two art internships while making time to create new artwork and exhibiting them wherever I could. Anything I could do to create an impressive artistic resume.

I started living under this notion that I could sleep when I was dead. And it's not surprising that my body started rejecting the intense unrelenting pressure I was putting on it. On top of that, I faced letter after letter of rejection from every graduate art school I applied for. Not only was I not getting a full ride scholarship – I couldn't even get a school to admit me into their master's program. I started experiencing tremendous anxiety and panic attacks. For a year I lost my ability to regulate my own breathing. Everything in my being was out of rhythm. I didn't know anything about anxiety or the physical side effects it caused. To illustrate the ridiculous level of how I was living fully unaware of what was happening to me, I cashed out my savings bonds from my childhood believing I was having strokes and thought my life might be cut down at any moment. I took the money and purchased tickets to go visit my mother in Florida where she was now living with her boyfriend, thinking some rest would help me recover. I thought for a moment I could run away from the pressure and fear of failure but it followed me unrelenting. I was still striving to find a way to manifest my own destiny. It wasn't working. I couldn't get relief from the symptoms I was experiencing no matter where I was.

After returning I decided to go to the doctor and see what was going on. They gave me a checklist to see which symptoms I was there for and I didn't leave one unmarked. All of them. The Doctor looked at my chart and looked up with curiosity. He asked me how much caffeine I was drinking after I told him I worked at Starbucks as a barista. My coffee intake at the time was more like an IV extension. He laughed at the number of Venti's I was drinking a day and showed me his tiny cup of coffee that he said was the maximum suggested amount. I had hardly been in the room with him but a moment and he diagnosed me with anxiety. He said I had two options; I could get medication in which he said just knowing I had some on hand could in itself alleviate some of the anxiety I was experiencing with panic attacks. Or I could make some drastic changes in my life after I had explained to him how many hours a week I was working and how little sleep I was getting. He believed with some adjustments I could rid myself of these afflictions. I don't remember his name but I do remember his face. I remember looking in his compassionate eyes and knowing what he was saying was the advice I needed to hear and it was time to make some drastic changes in my life.

5
NEW LIFE

It was time to let go of some of the things I was contending for that were not viable or life giving anymore. The dream I was working so hard for had become life taking. Being an artist was the only identity I had but it was time to lay down what I believed was the only way to become known. My mother's words came back to me, I should have gotten a degree in business. Shortly after this I applied for a job in accounting. I had resigned to working in a space my co-workers and I called "The dungeon." I sat every day in a tiny cubical with papers stacked knee high. I was still experiencing crippling anxiety and no direction other than some paintings I was working on in my home studio. Trevor and I had been settled into a small apartment near the Twin Cities where he was working at a school. Conversations about starting a family became dominant and suddenly settling down didn't sound so bad. Having a family was something I knew Trevor had always wanted but I had a fear that I wasn't going to be good at it.

We decided to start a family and it took much longer than expected. A year went by and this dream started to feel out of reach for us too. In this season of longing I started walking with the Lord and praying for help and direction. I was utterly yielded to Him to make a way. This was a new place of dependency on Him as I knew I was powerless when it came to creation. There was no striving or manifesting this dream. It was being still and waiting. The striver in me couldn't work this out on my own.

At the age of 25, I became a mother and held our firstborn son. He was such an answer to prayer and a dream fulfilled. We purchased our first home and moved out of the cities and into the country near our hometown. I had never been around infants in my life and knew absolutely nothing about raising children. My doctor assured me there was no better training than on the job. We named our son Henry, and it wasn't until I held his small fingers and looked at his perfectly formed face that I discovered the miracle of life and unconditional love. In that moment of awe and wonder I never wanted to be anything more than a mother for the rest of my life. This was a surprise to my dear patient husband who had only ever heard the opposite from my mouth. We had many negotiations about how we would start a family and I would be the one with the career and he wanted to be a stay at home dad. But just like that – in the hospital room on March 21st, 2010 I was made new by love once again.

By this time my anxiety and all of its side effects were minimal and I was starting to experience a new calling as a mom. Something of a natural rhythm was findings its way into my heart. I was able to find some part-time work while we built our lives and let our roots grow down into our small community. We decided it was time to check out a church we had heard a lot about nearby and soon found ourselves at home. It was a large church, which was so far out of our comfort in size and scale. The music was loud and there were occasional hands flying up in the air and this new concept of adult baptism I didn't know was a thing. With zero contexts and an entirely new expression of Christianity I was leery. It was a stark contrast to all of my experiences so far. Where was the stained glass? The burning incense? They were replaced with a dark room, stage with lights, a fog machine and a coffee shop. Even though I was hesitant to embrace this level of newness, I was excited by the amount of people gathering and singing together. There was a sense of belonging that made me feel at home in the sea of people gathering to worship.

Month after month, sermon after sermon my understanding of who God was started to change. Coming from an unchurched background with such limited exposure I had no theological understanding that most of the Bible was anything other than a collection of myths and stories. A book to inspire rather than inform us of historical events that took place such as the creation story, Noah or Moses. The pastor at this church had such a reverence for scripture and made it so applicable. He believed every word of the Bible to be inspired by God in His sovereignty. His unshakable belief that the scripture should be believed as it was written convicted and challenged all of my previous beliefs. This changed everything. He also made everything about God relational. I had really only known God through my own experiences but it hadn't been talked about that way from a pulpit.

Trevor and I both fell in love with Jesus in that church and suddenly that loud music become something we couldn't get enough of and the hand raising people became ones that I admired instead of judged. I was jealous of the way they swayed abandoned and free. One Sunday I watched as Trevor jumped to his feet to join a crowd of people getting baptized. I hesitated to join him because I had gotten baptized at the Lutheran Church in my teens, but this time I wanted to do it out of love and not fear. We stepped into the warm indoor water and the lead pastor, whom we had never met, took me by the hand. In a moment that stood still as thousands of people looked on at us from afar, the pastor turned to Trevor and said, "Take care of her," and plunged us beneath the baptismal waters.

I didn't feel any different coming up than I did when I went down. I thought maybe I would have some kind of feeling of transformation but I was the same. The only thing that defined that moment for me were the words spoken to Trevor. It felt really out of place at the time. When I revisit the scene, it's like God was speaking to Trevor as a father would speak about his daughter. Take care of her Trevor. The words I never got to hear a father say. This wasn't a wedding but it was a declaration or a promise to each other and before God and His bride that we were ready to walk into a deeper intimacy with Him.

Trevor tells me often as we look back at our lives together after being married 19 years now, he still feels like maybe his sole purpose in life was to love me. When I think of the love

Trevor has given me I believe it is Christ's love I'm experiencing. The same way that I heard His voice that day through the pastor baptizing us. When we love, we are experiencing the presence of God every time.[1] Trevor's love has been the testifying love of God in my life.

6
THE LIES WE BELIEVE

We enjoyed being parents and watching Henry discover new things every day. We couldn't believe how fast he was growing and decided it was time for another addition to our family. I had a textbook pregnancy with Henry and hadn't anticipated the possibilities of miscarriage. But nine weeks into our second pregnancy, just days after publically announcing it, we lost our growing miracle. It was so devastating I didn't know how to process the amount of grief I felt losing that little life inside me. I carried so much shame and fear into our next pregnancy I didn't have a moment where I wasn't waiting for something to happen. When our daughter Charlotte was born, I sobbed uncontrollably as she took her first breath. These moments were priceless, where fear was cast out by perfect love. Balancing fear and love continued to create a beautifully chaotic world as we navigated the challenges of parenthood.

I was 30 when we discovered we were going to have a third child and the trauma of our miscarriage caught up with me in my first trimester when I got sick. I was afraid of doing anything to treat my fever symptoms so I went against a nurse's advice to medicate and let my flu pass on its own. Later I was researching fevers during pregnancy and learned how dangerous it could be in development, particularly the first trimester. Anxiety and overwhelm launched me into a depressive state even long after our son Arthur was born healthy. The weight of striving to be God and manage life around me was taking its toll. How quickly I always seem to pick up that mantle. I was tormented with shame and the fear of making the wrong decision. I couldn't shake the idea that if I had done something different, maybe I wouldn't have miscarried. I was convinced I had put our baby in danger by not taking the doctor's advice and treating a fever which could have had long term consequences for our son. I hated myself. There was an underlying narrative of self-loathing surfacing and I was living in constant fear of failure. I was looking for the narrow straight path which I perceived again to be a road where every decision I made had to be the right one. The perfect one that had no margin for error, especially mistakes that could hurt people – people I love.

Even though I loved being a wife, a mother and I loved the Lord with all my heart, I still felt like I wasn't enough. I had so many shortcomings I started thinking that it was possible that God had little to do with me. The spirit of fear became much louder than the Spirit of God in my life. I was so ashamed of how hopeless I was feeling I couldn't tell anyone about it. On the outside I looked like I had it all together. People would often comment to me about how perfect I was. If they only knew! I was newly self-employed and had a photography business and had picked up my artwork again with occasional sales and commissions. But in the shadows and the midnight hours, the dark places where I was prone to wander in despair, I found myself asking God night after night again to forgive my sins. The same prayer I had when I was 12 years old, believing there were some sins in me that were unforgivable. That I was so stained by my imperfections that I wasn't worthy to be loved. There were some mistakes I had made that even the blood of Jesus couldn't amend.

It was early in the morning and I grabbed my phone with two little ones running around and one sleeping in my arms. I noticed an unread message from a friend and it said, "I feel like you're worried about something..." it went on to name almost word for word the prayers and cries of my heart that I had uttered to no one. Only to God. She wrote it exactly as I had been travailing in it but she assured me that everything was okay. Everything I was worried about was fine. She brought up the number four as it was standing out to her as she noted the time with no idea why that would be important to me. As I scrolled through the message I was undone. I had been telling God we wanted to have a fourth baby but I couldn't do it out of fear of what could happen. In that instant I felt chains break off of me. I had been cloaked in so much fear and held captive by it that I was letting its distortions and lies enslave me. It was stealing and killing the joy from my life and calling me to this unyielding darkness.

It felt like I had received a direct text message from Christ Himself through this beautiful friend who thought I would read her message and think she was crazy. That one moment changed the trajectory of my life. I didn't know that God could or would do something like that for me. It felt like He really cared about my suffering and my prayers. Susie Larson, radio host and author says, "The storms reveal the lies we believe and the truths we need." In that moment, the storm I was in revealed that I had God all wrong. I perceived Him to be distant and someone who I had to seek out if I wanted to have a relationship with Him. It was all determined by my ability to seek and find Him. But this, this felt like He had come for me and pulled me from the depths of the sea when I had surrendered to being swallowed up.

He also reminded me once again, there are some things in this world I cannot control, but there is nothing too out of control for Him. Maybe I wasn't created to be perfect and not make mistakes – I had to accept that imperfection was a part of living in my dust body. But that didn't mean that God couldn't or wouldn't be with me or love me whether I did it right or wrong. I was starting to see that He was in it all. It started to become clear to me that the greatest weapon against my relationship with God was to believe that I was still a sinner. That I was too far from the grace of God and too dirty to be wiped clean. Where was this lie still coming from and why couldn't I rid myself of it?

Not long after this our family started tasting the fruit of fellowship in a smaller church community. The word home always comes to me when I find myself in places with people where I feel I belong. This was home. These people were home.

Our days were now spent child rearing, participating in community groups, volunteering and walking out our faith in new ways and making new deep relationships. Part of me was still feeling like a fraud because everyone always seemed more Christian than me. I knew nothing about scripture still. Even though we had been in the church for years now, I felt like I had only gotten a small serving of the Bible. I really wanted someone to help me read the Bible as a whole because I didn't know where to start or how to start. I wanted to know more about God especially after the way He had spoken to me so personally. This was all a new revelation of who God was.

During this time a friend of ours got diagnosed with brain cancer. It came as a shock to all of us. We were visiting and she told me how she was reading through the Bible because it was something she was determined to do in her lifetime at least once. The next time I saw her she was radiating joy because she had finished. I wanted what she had in that moment. There was something of the joy and hope she was carrying even in the midst of her battle. I still only had my one verse memorized and I was ready to see what else the Bible would have for me beyond the narrow way. In my mind, if I knew more about the Bible I would be able to finally have that last piece of knowledge that would make me a good Christian. There was still a blockage in my identity that made me feel less than. I was so inspired by her I purchased the *Bible in a Year* book and set out my goal.

Every time I thought about starting it however I had a random thought of some friends from high school. I didn't understand why I was seeing their faces but it happened so many times uninvited I finally considered it might be something the Lord was bringing to my attention. At church we were in a teaching series called, *What If.* So I asked myself the question, *what if* God wanted me to invite these friends to journey with me through the Bible. They might say no but what if they said yes? This paved the way to how I started discerning when I believed God was speaking to me. Something we hear about in the Bible but seldom speak about in church and in our own lives. At least this was true in my own experience. God spoke to me through someone else, why wouldn't He want to speak to me too? This gave me the courage to speak it out instead of writing it off. When I reached out to my friends to see if they were interested in reading the Bible in a year with me, much to my surprise they all said yes. So there we were, a small group of biblically illiterate women setting out to read the Bible together.

I had no idea how many questions would arise and how many things I didn't understand as we worked through those pages every day. There were times I felt completely lost trying to understand parts of the Old Testament. I could not marry together the God I was reading about who seemed to encourage war, disease and death and I was paralyzed by the amount of bloodshed within the text. There were terrifying consequences for people, God's people, for making the wrong decision. He gets angry. He sends snakes to bite people. He gave Miriam leprosy for talking against her brother. He told Saul to wipe out entire nations including infants. What more would He unleash on a sinner like me? The striver inside was reeling with fear of God. I was so sickened by the thought of an angry Father and surmised that maybe the bad things that happened to me in my life, were because I had done something terribly wrong or offended God in some way.

Many things in the New Testament didn't make sense either. There were conflicting messages in some of the verses that went against the things taught or practiced in the church we were in. I was blindsided when I read, "Women should learn quietly and submissively. I do not let women teach men or have authority over them. Let them listen quietly. For God made Adam first, and afterward he made Eve."(1 Tim 2:11-13) I had been raised by a single mom. I didn't have a vocabulary around submission or quiet learning. What did that even mean? Second, I was in a church with a female pastor. What did they know that I didn't know?

I was still creating paintings of Christ when I read through Exodus where God was commanding people to not make any images in the form of anything in heaven above or on earth beneath or water below. I was jolted by fear that my artwork was unholy and punishable. I was trying to understand right and wrong and just wanted to please God. I asked the leaders of the church to help me process some of these questions and they replied by saying they were just like me, trying to figure out what God wants from them the best they could. This was frustrating for me on so many levels. It was a genuine loving response, but it left me feeling alone and lost in a world I didn't understand. On one hand I was being told that every word in the Bible was inspired by God. On the other hand, I was confused by the way we were responding to the word as a church that seemed out of alignment with what I was reading.

There were so many challenging concepts that we weren't talking about. How were we okay with all of these beliefs we were telling one another to adhere to on a Sunday morning, when it seemed to me that there was no one way to interpret the Bible. No one would say that but it was starting to be implied by the way I could not get any one answer. I was so unsettled by hearing that some things are black and white and others are grey all over. Who determines what is black, white or grey? I wanted someone to show me the way the truth and the life and I thought the church was the only place that could help me do this. I could not have foreseen what would unfold in the years ahead that would re-define my understanding of the word completely. That year I did finish reading the Bible but I had more questions about who God was than I had before I started.

7

UNRAVELED

Upon the arrival of our fourth child, I was running full steam again. My small business in family photography had taken off and I had more work than I could keep up with. I was stretching myself thin again at a great expense to my loved ones. I had this new idea that God was bringing me all of these opportunities and I needed to say yes to every single one. If He was sending them, He must think I have the capacity to do them all. My anxiety and overwhelm resurfaced and heart palpitations and panic attacks were full force as coffee intake was immeasurably high again. I was up all day with the kids while Trevor worked and I was editing photos at night until two or three in the morning most days. Trev would often ask me to slow down to which I would laugh. Did he not realize how much work there was to be done? He would tell me he wanted more time with me but that was the last thing on my mind. Work and children were first and after that I had little to give. But if anyone else needed help with anything, I always seemed to be able to find time for them.

Trevor quietly and without condemnation watched me do what he had seen time and time again. Crashing and burning. I loved being a mom more than anything in the world and enjoyed every second of watching my kids grow. I let go of all my ambitions to paint and make a name for myself through my art. I just wanted to be there for my family. However my inability to slow down made it hard for me to be present for anyone, especially Trevor. In 2017, at the age of 33, not surprisingly my world imploded. I lost a friendship with someone who had felt like a pillar in my life at the time and I was hurting in ways I had never hurt before. We had a health crisis with one of our children, I lost a close family member and things in our marriage were getting exposed that needed help. On top of all this our house flooded and the wreckage around me was a portrait of my life and the destruction going on inside. I hit my breaking point.

It was at this moment I looked at where my life was and found no foundation. Not in my marriage, my children, my church, my business or successes. It was the darkest and most isolating year of my life. I couldn't eat or sleep and experienced adrenal fatigue. All I could do was ask myself the question, *how did I get here*? Someone at church looked at me one Sunday and said, "You look like the light has gone out from your eyes." I couldn't hold up a façade anymore. She saw on the outside what was going on inside. I replied with honesty and told her I was struggling with anxiety and depression. She laughed thinking I was being funny and walked away. There didn't seem to be anyone around that knew how to enter into this heaviness with me. Not to the depths I was swimming. So often when we see someone drowning in pain we stand at shore telling them they are in too deep. We want them to swim back to shore.[1] Unresolved pain launches an automatic search for relief.[2] I felt like that lost girl behind the closed door again waiting for a search and rescue team. As we process pain, we look to see if anyone is with us in our time of suffering. If we believe we are alone and the pain exceeds our mental capacity, we are traumatized.[3] I didn't have anything to hold onto through this storm and I was disassociating from the world. I was unraveled. But in the unraveling I started to see something I had not seen before.

Many years ago my mother tried to teach me how to crochet. I clumsily wove together a string with her direction and after an hour or so I had only accomplished a frustrating amount of knots. Still, I was feeling pretty proud of what was holding together. Out of nowhere my son ran by and grabbed the string and pulled as he hurried past - undoing each knot one by one before my eyes. This was how my heart felt day after day. Like the string that had been holding me together was pulled and suddenly everything inside came apart. I was trying to blame others for how I had gotten to this point but here I sat unraveled and the only one that I could point the finger at was myself. I started to see how much I had hurt my husband over the years and not perceived his needs but demanding he meet all of mine by prioritizing my time above his. All the ways that I was driving our picture perfect life into the ground by not slowing down. All the people pleasing I was doing and my inability to say no to anyone for fear of rejection.

There is a story in the Bible that I was thinking about a lot during this time where Jacob wrestles with a man from evening until the break of dawn. Jacob got his hip wrenched out of socket but wouldn't let go until he got a blessing. One of the hardest things I was wrestling with at this time was how to see God in my life as I sorted my rock bottom moments past and present. It felt like I was in a standstill with the Lord and my hip was out of socket but I was still holding on to Him for more. Because I knew He cared about my pain, He had shown me that a few years prior in a powerful way through the text message from my friend. In the story of Jacob, God gave him a new name. A new identity. Jacob in return named the place he wrestled, "Peniel (which means 'Face of God'), for he said, 'I had seen God face to face.'"(Gen 32:30) God was about to give me a new name, a new identity and allow me to see Him face to face. Never to be the same again. But I was in a wrestle over my identity and it was an agonizing process of looking at myself. All of myself. Every hidden place and every hurting place that I had unknowingly been living from.

I was praying like my life depended on it, and it felt like it did. I started devouring stories of overcomers like Susie Larson and Sheila Walsh, brilliant authors, who knew the valley I was in and could testify to the power and love of God. I would wake up before our full house and read my Bible and ask the Lord to read it back to me and show me where He was in it. I would ask Him, where would you like me to read and He would say, exactly where you are. And every day I would pick up where I had left off and every single time there would be something on that page I needed to receive. His words became a theme for me, *exactly where you are.*

There was a road I would drive on regularly and every time I would pass a certain tree, a cloud of birds would emerge and fly over me. Mind you, the speed I was traveling was 70mph so the timing of this was impeccable. Every time this occurred I would think to myself, had I been one minute ahead or one minute behind I wouldn't have seen that. After many more times I started feeling the Lord reminding me again and again, you are exactly where you are meant to be, not a minute ahead or behind. He was deconstructing the striver in me. It was effortless on my end to be where I was in the present with Him. I didn't have to do anything to be there at the right time. I just was. The pain I was feeling started giving way to His presence. He was with me and I didn't have to do anything to find Him.

I met with a counselor to help me sort through this overwhelm I had been unable to manage. She was so helpful in asking good questions, and showing me how we can sometimes be more task oriented over people oriented. This resonated with me and started bringing self-awareness to my marriage. She also helped me lift up Trevor's voice to a new level of love and appreciation for the heart that he carried and his desire to simply be with me. Something I had taken for granted for so long. She always encouraged me to bring things to the Lord to see what He wanted to say about it which helped me find confidence in my ability to hear His voice and receive His gentle healing. She introduced me to the idea of grace – but this time grace for myself. She had recognized my inability to love myself and was concerned if I knew or would ever be able to fully know God's love for me. I would read about how we were called to love others as we loved ourselves. I could not understand what that meant because I was unable to know how to love myself well. How can you give something to someone that you have not yet received for yourself?

It was here in my weakest and most vulnerable moments God was reclaiming my heart and rewriting my story. As I was finding deep healing from Him, I started getting phone calls, spontaneous visitors and emails from people walking through incredibly hard times. Far worse than anything I had ever gone through. I had no idea why they were coming but something was happening as I would sit and listen to their stories. I would see myself in their suffering and would share in their pain. I wasn't afraid of going to that place. I was already there with them. Simply being together and listening to each other started ushering in healing and breakthrough, even joy. They weren't coming to me for advice. They were coming to be heard and seen. If trauma is experienced when we are alone in our pain and there is no one that is happy to be with us in that place, then a healing agency of trauma is togetherness. As we come together and share our weakness – suddenly we find strength. This isn't a new concept. The Bible says that God's strength is perfected in our weakness. (2 Cor 12:10) If that is true, why are we living from our own strength all the time? This is the paradox that continues to cause me to fall. We are taught to cover our weakness and keep it to ourselves. The problem with this is that it goes against our very design. Weakness isn't a place we should run from but a place we should live from. What does this look like? I believe it is vulnerability. When we are vulnerable with our own stories, others find safety to be vulnerable with their stories and this is where healing and transformation occur. Loving people in weakness is where we find strength and it's the birthing grounds for miracles. It's what brought me back to life and became my testimony.

8
THE CALL

I call 2018 our year of miracles. My counselor told me she was using our marriage story to illustrate transformation to her other clients by the way my healing was helping Trevor find himself. With her help, I came to the realization that Trevor had a really healthy sense of how to be present and orient our lives much better than I. I began to run everything by him to get his thoughts and opinions on my time management and commitments. Trust was growing through the safety we were both feeling and we started to find a new rhythm where we weren't always running on empty or in crisis mode. We came through stronger and more connected than we had ever been. He would constantly say how thankful he was that I was finally able to see things that he had not been able to articulate or things I hadn't been able to receive.

I was feeling really called to try to read the Bible again because I felt I had a pretty good understanding of the God of the word - but I still didn't understand the word of God. I was going to start deep diving into the Bible and this time whenever I was about to start, I felt the Lord say, "Not alone." The concept of not alone had started to weave its golden threads into my story so I decided to do a call out for anyone who wanted to go deep into the scriptures with me. To my surprise people said yes. In fact many people said yes. This time I was determined to not only read the Bible but to see the love of God on every page because this was His love story. It wasn't always easy to do but finding tools, commentaries, podcast, teachings and learning a great deal of historical context started opening the scriptures to me and everyone that came along for the journey. We worked through the challenging places and wrestled with the text, and I did my best to answer the questions that arose. It was so helpful to see that I wasn't the only one that had felt lost. Even people who had been brought up in the church and been in Bible studies their entire lives were telling me they felt they were understanding the Bible for the first time. Understanding His heart.

Author Jen Wilkin introduced me to the metanarrative of the Bible in her book *Women of the Word*. She explains how understanding each book of the Bible is part of a bigger story. When we zoom in on a particular chapter, we need to examine it in the context of the whole picture. If we don't do this, we limit our understanding and narrow our focus and lose perspective. She writes:

> Without the bigger picture, we can gain only a partial appreciation of what any individual snapshot is trying to tell us. From Genesis to Revelation the Bible is telling us about the reign and rule of God. Its topography

speaks of creation, fall, redemption and restoration in every vista.[1]

When I had first read through the Bible, I didn't have a map. I didn't know the topography. I was stuck in places and moments that didn't make sense because I was too focused in to see anything beyond a certain verse or narrative. Wilkin opened me up, not only to the bigger story, but how I could apply this to my own story as well. I had a creation story. I was coming out of a fall that sent me on a path towards redemption. This new season of healing I was in, I was finding myself in the greater story. I was finding myself in His story and others were coming along on the journey with me. There is a quote I love by Soren Kierkegaard that says, "Life can only be understood backwards, but it must be lived forwards." It had been impossible to see where God was in so much of my story, but I was starting to look back with more understanding of what He had been doing all along. Suddenly the darkest places and chapters of my life became the places where I came to know Him in greater ways than I could have ever imagined. With more perspective of my own journey, I was starting to see the bigger picture and He was redeeming every moment in perfect time. I was exactly where I was meant to be. It seemed as if the tears I had cried became wellsprings of life and living water. Not only for myself but for others He was gathering around me.

One morning I woke up with a word repeating itself in my mind, *seminary*. With such little exposure to the church up until this moment I had no idea what seminary was. A quick Google search informed me it was, "a college that prepares students to be priests, ministers, or rabbis." I had been feeling a call to ministry but it wasn't anything beyond an occasional thought. In sitting with the idea of seminary that day I laughed out loud. There was no way I could go back to school. In the next few months the pull towards searching for seminary programs was growing but I didn't tell anyone that I was entertaining these thoughts. I knew there was no way this would work with four little ones, being self-employed and my ministry commitments. Not to mention financially it would be impossible. The programs I was looking at were expensive and we were already drowning in our unpaid college debt. I also had no inkling as to what I would do with a degree from seminary and what that would look like. I decided to keep these thoughts to myself, lock them in a box and throw away the key.

A few months later on November 5th, 2017 while my husband was away hunting, I got an email out of nowhere from our pastor at the time. It read, "I would love to explore any potential options as it relates to seminary for you! Yep…seminary." Suddenly I couldn't hide anymore. There was that word again and there was no more denying that it was something He wanted me to seriously consider. I jumped in my bed and pulled the covers over my head and hid myself. *Seminary*? Me? I felt so unworthy of being called to do something that seemed set apart from the world and life I was accustomed to. I felt unqualified because I was still trying to grasp basic themes and concepts in the Bible.

After speaking with Trevor, he gave me a response I would hear from almost everyone I shared with, "you don't need seminary to teach the Bible." On one hand I really felt I did because I was terrified of teaching something incorrectly. The Bible study was growing and I was feeling the weight of responsibility to not lead people astray with my limited understandings. There were a few times I had spoken about something that challenged a belief someone held and I felt awful. I wasn't trying to break down beliefs; I was trying to find understanding together by asking questions and seeking answers in a community. I didn't know how much some people would be challenged through conversations or new concepts that would stretch them uncomfortably. I thought seminary would help me find the right way to read and interpret the Bible so I could make sure I wouldn't offend or contradict any one belief system. More importantly, I knew it was something God was calling me to. I usually know its God because my desire is to run the opposite direction to which I feel called. Jonah is someone I joke about often as the person I identify with the most in the Bible. It seemed too impossible to be a reality so I started to pray for God to make clear what He wanted because there was simply no way this was going to happen as far as I was concerned.

I had met with my pastor and talked about options. I called a few different seminaries to hear about their programs and I had absolutely no idea what to do with any of the information. By now Trevor had been on board enough to say that if I felt like it was something I had to do then he supported me. I was burdened with the heaviness of trying to navigate something I didn't really understand, especially knowing what it would take away from our family. One morning I said, "God I don't know what you want me to do! I have no idea where to go and what you're asking of me." A joyful laughter sprung up within me and I heard the Lord say, "You will know!" I don't know how to explain the peace that washed over me but in that moment I heard a promise that He was going to help me know where I should go and what I would be doing. And the playfulness of the laughter gave me anticipation that it would be blatantly clear. Laughably clear even.

The next few days I started thinking of a pastor friend of mine who I met as a barista. I've met many pastors over the years working as a barista – coffee must be an agency of the Holy Spirit. This dear friend was a genuine kind soul and I felt nudged to reach out to him and ask what he thought about me going to seminary. He graciously offered encouragement and said he would like to help me on this journey and would see what programs were available. He had been a great support of my artwork and wanted to see if there was somewhere I could enroll that would combine both. Something I had never considered. What program could exist where I could continue to pursue art and study theology together?

A month later I got an exciting phone call from this friend who said I wouldn't believe what he had come across. The very seminary he had graduated from in Minnesota had an artist-in-residency program that he had just learned about. This included a full ride scholarship plus an additional artist stipend. As soon as I heard this, I recalled the laughter and the promise that I would know what path to take. It seemed too good to be true, but less than a month later I was signing papers to receive the scholarship and become Luther Seminary's artist-in-residence. Eventually I was able to step away from my photography business, and start a three year journey of pursuing a master's degree with a Bible concentration.

This became an Ebenezer moment for me that I come back to time and time again in remembrance of how God helped me. In 1 Samuel we read the account of how the Israelites were getting defeated over and over again by the Philistines. The Lord eventually gave the Israelites victory through a thunderous voice from heaven that sent the Philistines into confusion. This was a miracle moment where the people of Israel wanted to remember how the Lord made a way. To honor God, Samuel took a large stone and placed it between two cities and called it Ebenezer, which means the stone of help. This also marked a moment in history for God's people where He started reclaiming the territory that the enemy had stolen.

I woke up one morning with a word that I had no understanding of and it moved from a thought, to a hope and a dream, to a reality. This Ebenezer moment still astounds me and it changed the course of my life. But first, there was more territory the Lord wanted to give back to me.

9

IDOLS

"No man knows his own heart. I do not know mine. Who knows what is really in my heart."[1]

-Gene Edwards

One of the first things that God started reclaiming in me was my identity by healing my heart and cutting away some of the lies I believed. Dr. Jim Wilder writes, "Traumatic events often bring a two-fold destructive legacy into a person's life – there is a wound and there is a lie, and people suffer because of both. Both need to be properly taken care of before a person can live from the heart that Jesus gave them."[2] I was starting to see a lot of wounds from my past that I wanted to heal from, but I didn't know how. I was able to identify many things that would often trigger big emotions in me, but I didn't know how to get to the root and get control over them. Shame was surfacing in new levels making me ultra-critical of myself. I felt like a piece of Swiss cheese with holes all over and they were more apparent than ever - parts of me with voids that I had been trying to fill. Now I was seeing them for what they were, places of my identity that were missing something. I was getting pestered with the words my counselor said to me, "I'm afraid that you will never in your lifetime be able to understand the love God has for you." We spoke about serious concerns surrounding ministry and what that looks like with someone who has a problem understanding God's love and how to love themselves.

All of these lies over my identity were coming into full view and I couldn't suppress them. I sat in her office one day and I said, "let's go after healing the trauma I have experienced." She cautioned me that I might have too much going on as I was about to start seminary in a few months. But I was desperate for freedom so she agreed. If we revisit the story of the Israelite's in 1 Samuel, we see Gods people divided. They had forgotten who they were and had been worshipping false idols and living a life apart from God. Samuel said to them, "If you want to return to the Lord with all of your hearts get rid of your foreign Gods..." (1 Sam 7:3) The nation turned away from the lies they had believed, the false identity they had been living under of who they were and whose they were, and when they gave all of their hearts to the Lord, He then changed their circumstances. So often, the Lord is more concerned with our hearts and the lies we believe before He will give us victory in our circumstances.

We live in a world of fixer uppers but sometimes God gives us a breakthrough by allowing us to breakdown. Then we can see the false idols we cling to. We want to solve the problems in our lives and in the lives of others. We want to know the right thing to do, when really God's desire is for us to be with Him so that we can learn the right thing to do. He will make our paths straight. (Prov 3:6) He knows what things need to be dealt with first. We get stuck trying to fix something that's happening now, but the reason why we're struggling is because it's often rooted in something painful from the past. So often these unhealed places create blocks in our ability to know His heart. He was expertly removing all the things in my heart that had created space between us.

Through being with Him and giving our hearts to Him, we find a love that surpasses all circumstances. When we are aligned with His heart, our hearts become whole, we see Him move in our midst like never before. Our identities and our value come from knowing ourselves through Him. The first thing He did in my life at this time was address something I had missed completely.

I was starting to get excited that God was going to make a way for me to focus on my artwork again. It was something I was ready to use to glorify Him. But one day I was praying and I felt Him prompt the question, "what would happen if you didn't ever paint again?" This caught me off guard. I was fixed on inner healing so a question or thought like this that would enter into my mind, was not something I took lightly. I thought about why He might be asking me this and what heart work might be attached to it. Then I got upset. What was He trying to say? It actually sent me into a fit. "God why would you give me a gift and a passion and take it away? Why would you ask me to put something down that makes me so happy and I use to bring you glory?" I kept going with tears streaming down my face. "God who would I be if I wasn't an artist? I would be nothing. I wouldn't have an identity." There it was. Once I said that I knew we had just uncovered a lie that had been hidden beneath the surface. He wasn't asking me to stop painting. But He was asking me why I was letting my painting define me.

Something broke off me that day that I have not picked up again. I was not defined by a title, a gift, or a set of skills. I had let something God gave me, become my core identity. It was easier to be known as an artist than it was to be known as someone He loved. Art and success had a value system in the world, love did not. If my talent wasn't at the center of who I was, what or who would replace it?

Something else He had to cut away during that time was the way I was counting on people to inform my identity more than Him. I had gone to the church and put all of my desires to know and be known by Him on the leaders and members of the church. I thought for a time, if I wanted to grow deeper in my faith, I needed their wisdom and knowledge of God to inform me of who He was, who I was. I needed to know what the right thing to do was so God could use me. My prayers everyday had been, "God, let my life be a living sacrifice to you." I desperately wanted God to use me and wanted to know how to live fully surrendered to His will.

Everything about the way I engaged in my relationship with the Lord was through my works. Everything in ministry on how to love others became about how I could best lay down my life to serve them. The more I could do for the kingdom of God and for others would define me and how special I was to Him. The holes I was carrying were there because I didn't know what love was or what love felt like from God and from others apart from my works. Not only that but I was lifting up everyone else around me and putting them on a pedestal of holiness believing that pastors and ministry leaders have some super anointing that makes them far closer to the Father than I could ever be. Which is why I was terrified to start Seminary. I shared these thoughts with my counselor and said, "I know nothing about the Bible, nothing about God. Why would God call me to this?" She looked at me and said, "Jessie, you are the perfect person for this. It's not about being qualified for seminary. Look at all the people in the Bible, they had no qualifications."

Someone during that time also said that God doesn't call the equipped but He does equip the called. This was in stark contrast to how I had oriented my beliefs in how to be a "good Christian." But it wasn't about being good or bad, it was about being loved. Only I could not fully comprehend this. One day I was in my car driving and I came to a four way stop. Suddenly I felt God present in the moment with me and it felt like He showed me my heart for the church and for the leaders were well intentioned. He was showing me grace and understanding of why I had built my relationship with him on their foundation.

He knew I was seeking Him, but in that moment He showed me a critical adjustment in how to seek Him first. His desire was to reveal Himself to me personally so that I would know His heart for me. I could see how I had substituted that deep place of intimacy with Him by putting others in that seat. I had idolized them in a way and built my foundation on them and their beliefs. The danger in that were the expectations I had on the leaders and the people of the church. What happens when we lift up the church to this level of perfection and performance but see someone falling short - judgement. This puts so much pressure and expectations on our leaders and when they have a crisis or make a mistake, an entire community is undone.

When my world crumbled and my marriage felt like it was unraveling, I was enslaved to shame because I felt I had fallen short in every way. I had no margin for error or grace and I feared people misjudging me. During a particularly convicting session I was asked the question why I feared judgment from others so much. I was then told that people who fear judgment are often ones who judge the most. I started checking my heart and thinking about places where I could be judging. I was still coming out of a season of hurt and betrayal from a friendship. There was bitterness in me and it had become toxic in my thinking. Sometimes consuming where all I could think about was the hurt this person had caused me.

One night I had a vivid dream where two messengers came to me with a word from the Lord and said, "Pray thanks to God every day in everything." I woke up feeling the weight of this dream and started asking myself where I had given up on gratitude. There was something in my heart that needed to hear this. I was so focused on the hurt in my life; I lost my ability to be present in all of the things that God had given to me and done for me. This dream and encouragement became an onramp to a new level of joy and chiseled away at the hardness in my heart. I started journaling and writing down everything I was grateful for. Day after day I challenged myself to look for gratitude beyond the everyday people and provisions that I was thankful for.

Soon I started looking at all the hurt from past relationships and the seasons that were the most challenging and found gratitude in them. I was seeing all my circumstances differently and bitterness gave way to joy in the most unexpected ways. I started realizing all of the good that came from those hard chapters and suddenly I recognized I wouldn't have traded them for anything. They were the very things that brought me closer to freedom and closer to Him.

When we are experiencing pain, fear, shame, judgement or bitterness we have lost our ability to live in our true identity and design. Our relational circuits shut down and we lose ourselves in our efforts to protect our hearts from being hurt again. God was revealing places in my heart where I was stuck trying to be enough. Sometimes to feel enough, I had to constantly measure myself against others. In doing so I didn't look at them through a lens of love, but a lens of judgment. A constant warring within myself and the striver within to be everything to everyone. To prove my value and my worth. I had to find my value through people I believed carried the authority to make that judgement on me. God wanted to be the one to give me my value and to define what value system I should measure others against. It looked nothing like the one I was using.

Once I was aware of this, I wish I could say transformation happened overnight but it was and is a long process of healing and living in relationship with Him and others who love me like He does to remind me of who I am daily. So often I think we get frustrated when transformation doesn't happen overnight or we slip back to old ways of thinking and feeling. But the truth is, it is a journey that is ever changing and we are always coming against new challenges and growing and maturing in wisdom and understanding. We miss out when we try to rush through the process of healing and doing the heart work. Restoration requires rest and it can't be hurried. I can't have rest or peace without Him. I'm not talking about sleeping or relaxing, although those are very important too. I'm talking about rest that comes from His peace and His rhythm. When I am running around trying to impress Him and everyone else with my performance and my kingdom fingerprint I don't leave enough time or energy to feel and heal.

At this time I didn't have a vocabulary or language to understand this feeling of not enoughness or where it was coming from. But God was surrounding me with people and mentors that He would place in my life to help me through this process. But it started here, where He removed the idols that were keeping my heart from Him. Then He taught me one of the most important lessons about judgement that has been a fundamental shift to my understanding of how we are called to love others as we love ourselves.

One by one He showed me how the things I would judge as bad or painful, He declared good. Or the people I accused or brought to Him in anger, He showed me mercy or declared them as His beloved, His anointed. Often when I do this, lots of the painful feelings associated with those memories or relationships turned to compassion and empathy. He would lead me to scripture that talked about loving our enemies and what that looks like when we are living from His heart verses living from our hurt. You must be compassionate just as your father is compassionate.(Luke 6:36) Story after story in the Bible I would read of the people God declared His most beloved who made some of the greatest mistakes. Even in their brokenness God still positioned them for greatness. There wasn't a formula for being able to judge a person on how good they were based on their works. In the story of King Saul and King David we see a struggle between two men that God favored with title and position. Both made horrible mistakes in their reign, but in the end God lifted up David and dethroned Saul. But only God held the authority to do so.

In, *A Tale of Three Kings: a study in brokenness*, Gene Edwards gives a glimpse behind the curtain of the anointed. He shows us how God will elect leaders who on the outside appear to be whole but are inwardly fractured, divided and rebellious. They are polished vessels who appear to be flawless and have the greatest value as far as the world is concerned. He calls these anointed ones, the King Saul's of this world.

In contrast, the King David's of this world are the anointed ones who spend years hiding in caves being broken. Brokenness becomes the agency of wholeness – allowing fractures to surface and mend. In the caves of our lives suffering often gives birth to humility where the broken vessels seek the will of God over a position of leadership. In the narrative Edwards cautions that

Saul lives in us all and "he must be annihilated… David could have been King Saul II – except God cut away the Saul in David's heart."[3]

Our hearts matter to God. And in the end, only God knows what is in our hearts and He will test them. Not to hurt us or destroy us, but He will do this to heal us and bring us closer to Him. Sometimes He will allow a Saul in our life to chase us into the caves where we will become a David. So much of our life is lived to avoid pain. But in our pain and suffering, our most broken moments can become the places of transformation. "How do we get the church to the point where we can face danger and hardship and be a transforming force in the world?"[5] How do we allow space for vulnerability and authenticity in the church where we welcome it to reveal what needs healing, and what does it look like to walk with one another through the process of transformation?

10

ENOUGH

In 2018, I had started journaling everything the Lord was speaking to me because I didn't want to forget the Ebenezer moments where He gave me a victory on the battlefield. But those victories weren't always moments where God was speaking loud and clear. Sometimes they were moments of silence and distance. Sometimes the space between hearing God and feeling God felt like a long hard winter. Something we know a lot about here in Minnesota. This fall I went to visit my grandparents who do a lot of farming. My grandpa was telling me about a large stone that almost took out the neighbors combine as he was harvesting. When he described the size of the rock in the field I asked him how on earth a rock that size appeared out of nowhere. He said that's what the frost does. It works them out of the ground to the surface.

These giant boulders can cause damage if they aren't removed. In the months leading to seminary I was doing a lot of trauma therapy. There were weeks and months that God felt distant and cold and these quieted moments pushed new stones to the surface.

August 28th, 2018

It's been a week since my last appointment where I discovered a "conditional" response to fear and anxiety situations but also to blessings. It all came back to this fear of failing or not doing enough. Needing to achieve to be loved and to love myself. Fearing I won't be able to live without disappointment. It's translated into my relationship with God and the way He speaks to me, causes self-fulfillment, not being able to wait on him, and the way I can't receive his love & blessing.

I was feeling insecure by not being able to understand what love was apart from my works. I was being stretched and pushed into new territory and it was a hard place to be. I was frustrated because I couldn't force healing to happen. It was hard to trust His love for me because I feared rejection or disappointment would come with it. I asked the Lord how I could have more love, more of Him especially when I didn't feel like He was there. He said, "I'm always with you." This might sound laughable to you, but I hadn't really considered that. I thought to be with Him, I had to reach for Him. So I asked Him, if He is always there, how could I be more present with Him. He said, "When you are loving others, you are loving me." Here I thought

I needed to lock myself away in prayer like a nun in a cloistered abbey to be able to experience Him all day. Being present with Him was actually being present with the ones around me. In loving my husband, my children, and my neighbors I was experiencing Him.

Some of the boulders that I had perceived as massive obstructions and blocks in my way, were becoming Ebenezer stones. God was using them to build a new solid foundation in me. Then I had a memory come to mind of myself as a little girl. We had this giant boulder in our yard and I would make a game out of running fast and jumping over it. One day I tripped on the stone and twisted my ankle painfully. As I asked the Lord why this memory was coming back to me, He said the stones in my life that had caused me to stumble, were going to be the stones I would stand on. "The stone that the builders rejected has now become the cornerstone. This is the Lord's doing and it's wonderful to see." (Matt 21:42)

I started seminary in September with a course on theology with a beautiful professor who called herself a Luthercostal. She was a passionate blend of the Lutheran and Pentacostal tradition. There were many denominations represented, but the majority identified as ELCA (Evangelical Lutheran Church in America). I was in the minority as a nondenominational student, affiliated with the Evangelical Baptist denomination. This gave me a unique lens and perspective in conversations throughout my time at Luther coming from a rather conservative community of believers. But it also caused many more boulders to come to the surface and challenged the core of my faith. I felt I was often one of the only students in any given class that had not grown up in a church, as a pastor's kid, on track to becoming a pastor, or currently pastoring a church. When we would go around the room and introduce ourselves I would get comments or have people come up to me after class astounded that I would be in seminary just to study the Bible. I had asked the Lord once why I was in seminary and I remember a clear response, "It's about what I am going to do *in* you." I knew it wasn't going to be a clear title or position and it was something I could not yet see or know. There was always a tension of feeling like I didn't fit in because everyone else seemed to belong in this atmosphere and knew the language. I didn't.

During my first week of what we called intensives, I was starting to be challenged by some of the teachings and comments from other students. We had been talking about the origins of atonement theories around the cross and what Christ's death accomplished and how these understandings had trickled into all modern day preaching. One of the main schools of thought around this is the notion that God paid a price for us as sinners. This associates His forgiveness with negativity and our unworthiness. Both the professor and a student commented on how this idea floods the Christian music market. I am a big fan of Christian music and it is all we listen to in our home. I was shocked to hear what they were saying and wondered what this conversation had to do with my music. I started listening closely to the words in the songs I was singing to try to see if I could find anything that sounded negative. Any songs that made it seem like we need to earn God's love or that we owe Him something beyond what Christ paid for us because of our sinful nature.

Suddenly one of my favorite songs came on. I was enjoying it and signing along thinking, every part of this song is true until I heard the words come out of my mouth in a completely different way. The chorus cried out that we can't earn God's love and don't deserve God's love. Pause. We don't deserve God's love? Is that true? I had been singing that line over and over again believing with all of my heart it was true. I am a sinner and I don't deserve God's love but He gave it to me anyway. That makes Him a good Father, but I am still a sinner in need of a savior. Right?

September 2nd, 2018

Then suddenly I saw it. The lie. We do deserve his love. I got home and told Trevor about this revelation. I said Trevor, they are singing that we don't deserve God's love. He said, "We don't." with confidence. I know right!? But that's the lie. We do. We do. It would be like saying to our kids they don't deserve our love, they can't earn it. But of course they do! Our love for them is not attached to their behavior. Nothing they can do will ever separate our love for them.

My love for them is woven into my DNA, I carry pieces of them in me and me in them. Nothing can separate my blood from theirs and that is what the blood of Christ does for us. Why would God send his son to die for us if we didn't deserve it? Why would he go through the trouble if he didn't love us fully and completely? We need to change the way we as his children understand his love because if we believe we don't deserve it we are reflecting that onto others that will never want to enter into a relationship with him, a God with conditional love.

I was starting to understand what they were talking about. Soon my ears were hearing this language in many songs and a lot of the preaching and teaching I was listening to. Trevor and I went to a Christian conference around this time and they had a breakout session about evangelism. They were using the same language of how much we don't deserve God's love. We inherited a sinful nature and Christ came to take on our sin as punishment because God required justice. This was the message people need to hear so they could be saved from their sin. But the language of love was missing. The heart of God who sent His son to die for us because of love was missing. Instead of it sounding like a God who wants to be in relationship with us, it sounded like a God who needed a payment. But what if God's forgiveness was associated with His love and not His justice? How would this idea change the way we look at ourselves? How would this change the way we love ourselves and love others? We love because He first loved us. I was starting to see why I was always so focused on getting things right and being enough for God. The striver in me was serving a God who needed me to make sacrifices, to serve Him, to pray more, to be perfect and blameless for Him to use me. But the idea that He loved me and that was enough was starting to feel true. It just wasn't the language Trevor or I grew up with or heard in the churches we belonged to. Even my prayers, "Use me God," were starting to feel like the wrong prayers. I was thinking about what kind of relationship that would be with our children if that was the motivation of their heart, to be used by me.

The transition to a full-time student was intense. I was juggling too much as a stay-at-home mom between studying and attending courses that required lots of concentration and time, trying to paint and fulfill my artist in residency status, and our Bible study transitioned to a non-profit to which I was CEO. We were invited to go to Africa on a mission trip and another friend had shared with us that they believed the Lord was showing them we were being called to move into full-time mission work as a family out of state. I was being pulled in too many directions and I wanted clarity but got silence. I felt like I was standing at a cross-road with no map on where to go. The accusations that would linger in my ears at night were often around trusting God. Did He really say that? Does He really love you? Are you really of any value to Him? Is He really a good Father?

In the silence of waiting for Him to make my path straight I questioned everything I knew about him night after night. The more I studied the Bible, the more I learned that there was no single way to interpret the text. Because we all carry a different lens we will all have a different understanding of who God is based on our experiences, gender, ethnicity, geographical locations, and social status. My theology professor made a statement in class one day that if you were to take the church of the Bible and compare it to the church today, there wouldn't be one thing in common. I was starting to feel like the very idea of truth was a lie. What is the meaning of truth if it's different for everyone? How will I ever know who I am if I can't figure out who God is?

We caught up with some friends one night and they were asking about our lives and what we had going on. We were sharing with them all of the things that were set before us and what we were discerning. Trevor was open and willing to do whatever the Lord may be calling us to but the emotional roller coaster of seminary and all of this God-talk was causing me to question everything. Especially myself. I shared this with our friends and they asked a great question.

December 15th, 2018

I was telling them how God has given me a buffet of things that I know He is calling me to. James replied with these words that struck my soul. "Did God put those things before you, or did you put them there?" I couldn't answer, he was right. Were there things there that I had loaded on the menu that God had not? I knew with the stress and anxiety I was suffering it was possible. So the next month I sought out a reset button. A fresh start. It seemed to me that maybe God was just seeking my belief in Him. Doesn't matter what he is calling me to.

I went on a fast from fear and started realigning myself with only the things that were before me that I knew I was called to focus on. I said no to all the other things that were giving me anxiety like the mission trip. I felt horrible laying things down or saying no but once I did I had so much peace. I didn't feel that I was disappointing God by not doing everything that was before me that had potential to be a good thing, a God thing

This made space for a little rest and peace to flow over me as weight lifted off my shoulders. I focused on my family, seminary and our small budding Non-Profit which was full of wonderful friends and made for some of my most cherished memories as we gathered together weekly. I was holding onto the words God had spoken to me that being present through loving others was still experiencing Him. And it was and I did. Still working with my counselor I was desperate to rid myself of fear, anxiety and performance. As we entered into the New Year the Lord revealed himself to me as I sat praying in the early morning hours.

February 1ˢᵗ, 2019
I was praying and I heard the Lord say, "Look Up Child." I looked up and stared at the ceiling. I imagined Christ on the cross before me and I was so overwhelmed I turned away and I had a reaction in my

heart that unearthed something. "Not Enough." No God I can't look at you on that cross. I can't believe that you love me as you say you do. "Jessie why is that?" Because Lord, I'm not enough. There it is Jessie. There it is. Ever-present. But you are enough.

Later I turned on my phone and listened to Susie Larson who had become a mentor to me through her radio show. She said she had been woken three times in the middle of the night with someone on her heart that needed to cancel a trip but it was hard because they didn't know how to say no. It spoke right to me and reminded me of Africa because every now and then I would still think about it and hope that I hadn't made the wrong decision. Suddenly she popped up again doing a live broadcast. She said that morning she had been given another message to someone watching, a woman like so many, that feels like she isn't enough. In all areas of her life she isn't enough. But if she could stop believing these lies then God could do something so amazing through her. If she started praying bold prayers because she is enough to deserve these prayers then she could break free.

I sat with those words and weighed them against my life and asked myself the questions, Do I feel not enough as a Mom? Yes. As a wife? Yes. As a friend? Yes. As a daughter? Yes. As a child of God? Yes. As a seminarian? Yes. In all areas of my work? Yes. *Not enough* was the lie and bondage keeping me stuck in this reoccurring theme. A stronghold that was ruthless and cunning. I asked the Lord what God sized prayers have I forsaken out of fear and unworthiness? What kind of prayers would I believe for if I felt enough to deserve them? This lie that was woven into my heart was about to be pulled out. I started praying audacious prayers to God and held on to this new identity as one who was worthy of such hope. God gave me the verse in Joshua about being strong and courageous and not being afraid to remind me that He was with me. He drew my attention to the story of Moses when he was too tired to lift up his staff. The Lord wanted me to know I didn't have to be strong; He wanted to be my strength. I was trying to do everything on my own to know what direction He was leading me all the time. He was asking me to let go. Teaching me how to let Him show me the way. "The Hardest thing that God has to train His people in – is to wait in expectancy. Because prayer is all about doing something too large for ourselves so we have to do it in dialogue with Him."[1]

I was always stuck living so far ahead of myself trying to know what the next step was, I was missing out on all the incredible things God was doing in the present. Healing happens when we are present with Him and present within ourselves. When I wasn't stuck in the offenses of the past, or trying to navigate my future I was able to focus on the obstacles that the frost was pushing up. Clearing the path and making a way for the harvest. There is something about this process for me that looking back I can see the beauty and timing of seasons and how God used a winter season to make way for new life to push through the ground. As it grows it turns into a harvest and then a feast. This was the metanarrative of how my story was part of a greater story, His story.

11

FACE TO FACE

I had just finished my first year of seminary when we unexpectedly sold our house and were living with family while we were on the hunt. This level of uncertainty as to where we were going to live and put down roots was crippling. The housing market was incredibly hard and we couldn't get anyone to take any of our offers for a home. We spent the summer with my in-laws juggling a household full of kids and trying to navigate our next chapter again. Something I was working hard not to do but in this situation it was inevitable. We had no home. Being in seminary I was surrounded by people with incredible call stories to ministry. Many of them were willing to go anywhere in the world that they felt called to. It was inspiring to me. We were willing and more ready than ever to go wherever the Lord wanted us to go but we still had no clear path. I was also struggling with a close relationship in my family that was hurting me. I tend to struggle walking away from any relationship but this one could not be avoided and it was painfully hard to put up a boundary. Instead of coming to God with prayers and diving into scripture to find some comfort I was angry with Him.

God will you just speak plainly to me? Will you account for why I'm hurting again? School was becoming a real struggle as we were diving into more history of the church and the denominational divides. I thought I would be painting a great body of work but I had little to no time for such things. I was struggling with the chaos of the move and trying to settle our family in the best we could as we were in transition. I guess that is how transition seasons feel - out of control. I was fed up. It seemed following Him was not an easy path but one that felt more like a rollercoaster of constant ups and downs, twists and turns. I don't like rollercoasters. I like the lazy river ride. My heart was tired of being in turmoil. Where are you in this storm?

November 2nd 2019

School has been such a struggle. It plants so many seeds of doubt and countless theologies in my head filling me with clouds of haze that fall over my mind disturbing my clarity of the truth of God. I find myself questioning the nature of Christ the most. Who do you say that I am (Matt 16:15). Is not so easily answerable after reading two-thousand years' worth of theology where every single theologian has answered that differently and still does to this day. From conservatives to progressives and everything in-between – what is truth? Who are the teachers of truth?

This entry reminds me so very much of the same lost girl who didn't know who she was and who she belonged to. Where substance abuse laid a heavy cloud of haze and confusion distorting the perception of who God was. A familiar villain. The one who accuses and confuses. But this time it wasn't a substance. It was religion. It was the church. It was this swinging pendulum of the left or the right side. The left side says to the right, you are not even a Christian and the right side says to the left, you are not even a Christian. In class, my favorite Bible verses that had gotten me through the hardest chapters where God spoke love and wisdom to me were the same verses that caused others severe trauma and terror.

I've stood in circles with born again Christians condemning anyone who hasn't received the Holy Spirit through baptism, and I've sat with Christians who cursed the very idea of being born again by saying, "I was already born once, I don't need to be born again." The Lutheran students joked about the Holy Spirit as the shy member of the trinity but come together powerfully through tradition, community and grace. Predominately the Pentecostals spoke in class about the power and glory of the manifestation of the Holy Spirit in their lives. But instead of loving each other and holding each other's stories I've watched and listened to people judge one another time and time again. Both in seminary and in the church communities I had been a part of. Whether it's the gift of tongues, prophecy or the Catholic sacraments – everything was categorized and separated through a lens of right and wrong. The questions I kept asking were the wrong questions. I had been looking for truth, the right way and finding nothing that I could build a foundation on.

I full heartedly thought seminary was going to reveal more of who God was. But I imagined it was going to be something black and white that I could finally know and feel confident in. By learning more about religion I was finding less of Him. I reflect on this time for our family as my Job season two where Job went from trusting God in his circumstances to not being able to see God anywhere.

Jessie DeCorsey
Course: The Book of Job
Writing Assignment #4 - Final
Luther Seminary

I have experienced different kinds of suffering in my life. The year 2017 was my Job year. I suffered losses so great I was unrecognizable to all who looked upon me. Even to myself. Yet in my suffering, I was surrounded with the presence of God and I was able to keep my eyes fixed on his strength and eventually persevered. But what happens when God is absent in our sufferings and our prayers are unanswered? Not long ago I was once again in a Job like season, only this time I didn't sense God in it. God wouldn't account for it. I felt hopeless, confused and angry. Instead of coming to God with humility, I approached the throne room with anger and raised fists. God became the enemy in place of my circumstances because ultimately God was the one I placed the blame. After all, he allowed this to happen to me. What kind of God would allow suffering to someone he loved? My conclusion, God must not love me. I think we have all felt this way at one time or another in our lives.[1]

The book of Job is my favorite because it covers the topic of suffering and faith. Not only does it get us thinking about why God allows suffering but why both wicked and good suffer alike. Suffering has no favoritism. It is gruesomely unbiased. It also contradicts the ancient doctrine and belief system of Job's time that you reap what you sow. "The Book of Job is, from the first chapter, the classical statement that a man's lot is not the consequence of his deeds."[2] Who living today cannot relate to the challenges we face in our own unjust suffering? Whose faith isn't put to the test when we face our trials and tribulations? We often turn to God and find silence. We seek answers and they don't come. Like Job we may even curse the day we were born and call for an audience with God to plead our case.

I had contempt towards God. I remember one morning reaching out in prayer demanding answers from Him. Why do you have me here? Where are you in the church? If you are real and good, why is there evil? Why have I experienced suffering in my life if you love me? Where were you then? Where are you now? There as I threw out my accusations I felt the lord whisper to me and offer me peace. I can't remember what it was but I rejected it. God I don't want your peace. I want you to account for all of the hardship I've faced in my life. For all the struggles and all the pain. I want your answers not your peace. Your peace has done nothing to prevent me from pain over the years. I was lamenting. All the work trying to heal had allowed a lifetime of trauma wounds to surface unresolved. All of this pain and questioning in the midst of the chaos around me was the perfect storm to bring about the greatest reveal of God. He answered me out of the whirlwind, just like He did for Job. Face to face.

Our family was attending a small church plant in a city nearby and one service they offered a healing prayer. I scoffed in my head at the idea of healing. I was sitting in the back of the church in bitterness. God – I don't want healing. I was giving Him my two cents on what I felt about Him and how the only thing that was going to heal me was an answer from His very own mouth to account for all the bad in this world and in my life. As people got in line for some prayer the worship team came to stage and started playing a song. It was a familiar song. So familiar and yet completely out of place as it was not one you would ever hear on a Sunday morning. It was the song, *To Make you Feel My Love*, by Garth Brooks. The year it came out in a movie, I played it on repeat every day. It was a song about the greatest love imaginable. The kind of love I was yearning for. It was the same year that Jesus came for me in my darkest most hopeless moment and walked me away from a path of destruction.

As soon as they started singing the lyrics I saw myself as that little girl sitting in her room behind the closed door. It felt like Jesus was there with me when I was listening to this song all those years ago but He was the one singing the words to me then.

I just didn't know it was His love I was hearing through this song but that is exactly what He was showing me as I sat in the church.

When the rain is blowing in your face
And the whole world is on your case
I could offer you a warm embrace
To make you feel my love

Those words stopped me and seized my heart. It felt like the whole world was on my case. Back when I was younger and now. It was like time synthesized and He was there embracing the lost girls.

When the evening shadows and the stars appear
And there is no one there to dry your tears
I could hold you for a million years
To make you feel my love

It reminded me of the stars and how I would experience His presence as I looked up at the night sky in wonder. I'd forgotten how much the stars spoke to me of His majesty.

I know you haven't made your mind up yet
But I will never do you wrong
I've known it from the moment that we met
No doubt in my mind where you belong

He was singing grace to me. He knew I was struggling to trust Him. He was assuring me that He is faithful. That He is a good Father. He was reminding me that I have always belonged to Him. Since the moment we first met, my star breathing God who knit me together in that secret place. I belonged to Him.

I'd go hungry, I'd go black and blue
I'd go crawling down the avenue
No, there's nothing that I wouldn't do
To make you feel my love

As these lyrics washed over me I could see Christ going hungry for me for 40 days. I saw him getting beaten and bruised for me. When I heard the words, I'd go crawling down the avenue I saw the weight of the cross pressing His body to the ground - for me.

The storms are raging on the rolling sea
And on the highway of regret
The winds of change are blowing wild and free
You ain't seen nothing like me yet

I had tears streaming down my face. He knew I was in a storm and everything felt out of control. But He was singing a promise over me that there was hope. There was more of Him again that I had not yet seen.

I could make you happy, make your dreams come true

Nothing that I wouldn't do
Go to the ends of the Earth for you
To make you feel my love
To make you feel my love[3]

Go to the ends of the earth for me. It felt like He had. It felt like He sent out a rescue team. The one I was always waiting for. It wasn't anything I had done to get Him to find me. In fact I had all but thrown in the towel and laid it all down. It wasn't my works or my faith or strength that had orchestrated this moment. It was all Him. In my greatest weakness He revealed Himself to me. In that moment I didn't want answers. I didn't care about answers anymore. I had His presence. I had Him. I didn't need anything else.

Suddenly every circumstance that was overwhelming to me was no longer filling the spaces between and the veil of confusion was obliterated. He loved me so much and He was always there. I was never alone. I had seen it with my own eyes. He was there with me then and He was there with me now. A theophany is something that occurs in the Bible when people encounter God face to face. When they encounter God they are never the same again.

Although this was only happening in my imagination the song was attached to a very real memory. This memory that was full of pain had now been experienced with an awareness of where God was with me. A new memory was made. A lot of the trauma I had experienced and was experiencing in this season was occurring because I felt alone. In that moment, God's perfect love filled those holes and the lost girl realized she was never really alone. Even though I had experienced God's presence in my life in many profound ways, I would constantly fall back into old faulty beliefs about Him when my circumstances got overwhelming. There was something about this encounter through a specific memory that Christ redeemed in a way that brought me closer to His heart and closer to my own. A place where the lie of being alone was confronted with the truth of being fully seen and the door that I was stuck behind was opened.

12

I AM YOURS

We finally found a house not too far from where we had been living and were settling in by late fall 2019. The kids were adjusting to life in a bustling neighborhood with many friends of all ages to play with. Trevor was working a job at Costco and helping out as much as needed so I could get through school. It had been months since my experience in the church and I still could not explain or put into words how transformational it was for me. I didn't know of anyone having an encounter like this but I was not the same person I had been. I experienced more healing in that one moment than I had in years of therapy. I had a new sense of my identity in Christ and even though I couldn't figure out who He was theologically, I had met Him through a song and a memory.

Shortly afterwards, I tuned into a podcast between Susie Larson and a trauma therapist from Minnesota, Stephanie Rossing, as they talked about triggers. Stephanie shared a type of attachment healing therapy called Immanuel Prayer. As she shared with Susie what the Immanuel Approach was, I was shocked to hear that it was exactly what I had experienced. Someone was putting words and knowledge around my Immanuel moment. She explained different types of traumas and how the brain works. She shared stories of incredible healing she was seeing within her field through the partnering of neuroscience and what we know about God as healer. This approach to healing invites God into traumas and wounding where people are being transformed by perceiving God with them in their pain. This leads to rapid healing as painful memories are metabolized. To do this it builds on joyful memories increasing the brains capacity to be able to handle the amount of painful memory that has to process to be healed and resolved. In my experience God used a familiar love song that brought me into a safe place to which we then resolved a painful experience. In her interview, Stephany shared intriguing stories of different ways Jesus would come into memories and heal them. At the end of the show she shared that she would be doing training in the Twin Cities area for anyone interested to learn more.

In no time at all I found myself sheepishly walking into a room of around 100 people and sat in the back at a table with some welcoming faces. Stephanie and her colleagues introduced themselves and taught us the basics of healing through Immanuel and we spent a great deal looking at scripture and how much God cares about the renewing of our mind and living a life of joy and connection. I reached out to Stephanie after the conference and she was able to get me in to see her 1:1. She embodied the love of Christ in her kindness and warmth and like a detective she had an eye for investigating root sources. She explained to me how we try to resolve our present overwhelms when sometimes we need to go to the root of them – which often traces back to our childhood. When we heal the younger parts of us, the adult parts automatically receive healing. This was opposite the approach to healing I had been going through previously as we were trying to put out the fires around my current situation. Stephanie was showing me how important it was to redeem my story. Through Immanuel Prayer time and time again Jesus would rewrite the script and throw out the old lies and narratives one by one.

I noticed immediate transformation. In fact it was more like a transfiguration – I was a completely new creation in a matter of months. I love this definition of the difference between being transformed verses being transfigured. "Transfiguration itself refers to a change in a form or appearance, and the root, transfigure, simply means "to transform into something more beautiful or elevated," so transfiguration is a specific form of transformation." [1] The difference I was feeling was noticeable to Trevor immediately as well. He could hear the shift in my heart language towards myself, our family and others. It infiltrated my studies and my papers because I was encountering the love of God in profound ways through prayer. In seminary I felt I was only encountering division and separation through religion. Love became the only thing I felt I could build a foundational theology on. It was the only thing that was undeniable about God. He is love. We, being made in the image of love are called to love each other. If we don't know how to love ourselves well, we will not be mirroring love towards each other, but we will be judging others as much as we spend time judging ourselves. We are so focused on getting it right we spend all of our time pointing out everything that is wrong with ourselves and others.

I started using Immanuel Prayer journaling as a way of connecting to the Lord in my prayer time and something quite extraordinary was happening. Throughout the day when I would struggle with heavy emotions or something would happen where I would feel overwhelmed, frustrated with myself, or not enough the triggers disarmed as quickly as they came. All the old nuero-pathways of striving and condemnation were like major highways from a lifetime of thinking this way towards myself. I spent my mornings with Jesus who was always happy to be with me and never judged me no matter what memories about my past we revisited but instead loved me perfectly. These memories were giving me new pathways of love. If I found myself on an old route, I would quickly remember a new path – and happily turn on my signal light and take the exit ramp towards self-love and grace.

November 2nd, 2019
The Lord spoke to my heart through the process of Immanuel prayer last week and it's really working. I'm truly finding joy in the smallest things that make me happy. When bitterness tries to come to me or anger, resentment or fear I talk to those thoughts and say....me and God have been talking and He says He's got it. I don't need to think about you anymore.

I always knew I was supposed to trust God with all of my fears and anxieties. I knew that I was supposed to capture my thoughts and choose joy. But Joy is not a choice. It is a fruit. As is love, peace, patience, kindness, goodness, gentleness and self-control. The fruit only comes if it's attached to the vine. I had too many attachment wounds that blocked my ability to trust God and to be able to know His love for me. Once I was able to attach to him the fruit was a product of that deep intimacy and relational joy we had together through the unconditional love I was experiencing. Attachment is what Wilder explains in the book *Renovated*, as the kind of love that would have us running into a burning building to save a child or face certain death and is the only kind of love that can take root in our character.[2] It's a kind of love that creates oneness and belonging with the one we are attached to. "The force that creates character is relational… we do not become human by thinking *about* people or God. Our brain becomes human by thinking *with* those we love in an attachment way."[3]

So often we are taught to pray to God but not engage in a true conversation with Him. Without the two way conversation we aren't getting the attachment to Him that leads to true transformation. We aren't able to become like Him. For me, I had a lot of lies in the way, and memories that needed healing before I was able to have enough trust in Him to receive anything He wanted to tell me. Our stories matter to God because our hearts matter to Him. This is why He is more concerned with healing our identities before He may heal our circumstances.

Imagine if He was more focused on our circumstances so that we were able to manage our lives spectacularly and didn't need to rely on His strength. Suppose He allowed those lies to stay in our hearts that were connected to distortions of who we are and who He is? That is why sometimes we go through winter seasons that push to surface things we believe about ourselves, others or God that need to be dealt with. Sometimes those rocks and moments that make us stumble and fall, become the very foundation we build on and invite others into to help them rise up.

Within the first few times of connecting to Jesus through this kind of prayer style, I would have this image of Him holding a small gift box with a large smile on His face. Time after time He would present this gift to me and I would look at it and wonder why He was showing it to me. Something in my heart knew that I wasn't ready to open it yet or that it wasn't time. After a few months He said today was the day. In my spirit I knew this was going to be a special moment. He was weeping. Jesus was crying. I hadn't ever imagined what it actually was like to watch Jesus weep but here He was. Like a sappy father watching his daughter on her wedding day. As a wedding photographer I have seen my fair share of sappy Dads.

February 23rd 2020
I didn't know why He was crying these tears over me so I asked Him, Lord why do you cry? He whispered through broken breaths. I've been waiting since the day you were born for this moment. I didn't understand what He was saying. This moment? Yes, the moment

where you would find your identity. I began to cry with Him. I wept as I understood what He was saying. I could see Him labor over me from infancy, hovering, loving me, and yet… I didn't know or understand His love. My identity hidden and concealed from me. (I was cherished and loved by my Father in heaven.) I could see, as a mother, how horrible that was for Him to endure. Like a parent who could only see their children from a far, unable to see one another and how glorious would that day be when the two became one. When the walls fell down and nothing stood between the lover and the beloved any longer.

Thank you I whispered. I had been longing to know you my whole life. Then I saw it. The box He's been holding packaged beautifully, small with a bow on it. I knew I was ready to receive it. He'd been showing me this box since I began Immanuel Prayer bursting at the seams like a man waiting to propose with great anticipation for this moment. But I couldn't accept it. I couldn't open it. I apologized. I just didn't know how to accept it. He waited, as He has always waited with patience and love, and the smile knowing that it wouldn't be too long.

I took the small package and opened it to see a small rolled up paper inside. It was empty. Lord its empty what does it say? I knew I needed to let Him speak through me and it would be written so I grabbed a pen and a piece of paper and as I wrote the words came out, "I am yours and you are mine." I kept repeating it in my mind and asked Him what He meant by this? Then the veil lifted and the Father's heart poured into mine. I could see that I had only been able to give the Lord my heart. I am yours. That was easy for me to do. Use me Lord, have your way in me, take my heart Lord it's yours. But until now I hadn't been able to believe that He says, "You are mine." I had denied the Fathers love but committed my heart to Him. I loved Him with my entire self but I never dared to believe that He truly saw me, truly knew me, cared about me, desired me. I had read about it! I believed it in my mind that it was true. But I hadn't yet seen it with my own eyes. I rejected the idea that I, unlovable, not enough, unworthy, insignificant, sinful, broken me was worthy of anyone's love. Especially His.

I sat and shared in His pain of a world who rejects His love by not ever knowing it, truly seeing it. It's real. It's not far away. It's more real than any love that we experience and yet so few of us are able to receive it. He's not interested in our theology, It's our hearts that He wants.

There it was, the words that will forever be etched on my heart. From this moment everything changed. I wanted everyone to know how real His love was. How much He desires to be known. How much He wants to show us His presence in our joys and sorrows. How much He wants to break down the walls that separate us.

> We are confident most Christians would agree with the reality that God is with us. Abiding in Christ is a good way to live – actually the best way to live. The fruit we bear in our daily lives will testify whether we are abiding in Christ. Sometimes we fail to enjoy living in an Immanuel reality due to distorted perceptions of God's character.[4]

I remember a few times many years ago, being with someone and telling them how much God loved them. But the words I spoke over them were empty. I didn't really know if God loved them. Because I hadn't yet been able to open the gift He had for so long desired to give me. His love.

Now when I am with others, I already know before they tell me anything about their lives how loved they are. I already know the fullness of their identity as someone God loves unconditionally. When I live from that place, I am no longer looking at people as right or wrong, good or bad. Im not weighing them on a scale of worthiness. I want them to know how much they matter to God. How much their life and every moment of their journey, their story matters to God. There is no place that we can go that can separate us from the love of God. The only thing that kept me from knowing Him was a false identity, but He was always there. Looking back now, I can see exactly where He was. How He paved a way and cleared the path so that I could give all of my heart to Him, and receive all of His heart for me. God says through His prophet Isaiah, "Build up, build up. Prepare the way, take the stumbling block out of the way of My people… I dwell with the one who is contrite and humble in spirit, to revive the spirits of the humble and the hearts of the contrite ones, those who are crushed into dust,." (Isa 57:14-15, my trans.) It was in my broken places that He built me up through revealing all the lies I believed and the truths I needed to know the fullness of His love.

13
TRUTH

"I was born and came into the world to bear witness to the truth. Everyone who is of truth hears my voice. Pilate said to Him, "What is truth."

-John 18:37-38

In February of 2020 I had just finished one of my first paintings during my artist-in-residency called *Tetelestai*. It was a project I worked on with a professor after taking a course of his on John's Gospel. I was moved by his teaching and the way he spoke about the cross through the lens of love. A refreshing interpretation of how to focus on the love that sent Christ to lay down His life for us, not the sin and judgement. It was the first week of March when I was able to drop off my painting on campus for installation. I was eager to hear the thoughts of other students and faculty. Then everything as we knew it would change.

I was never able to see the painting installed. In fact, I was never able to return to campus as a student. The Covid-19 pandemic struck our area and we sheltered in place. Courses were all transitioned fully online and the rest of the year I continued on while getting our four children through school at home as well. In addition to the pandemic our cities were burning following the events of George Floyd. I was grieving with all of the chaos and darkness in the world around us and the division of our people and nation.

It was an interesting time to be in seminary studying the history of the church and how it has transformed through the years. Because of the pandemic, people were not able to gather in person and found the church existing outside the four walls. A lot of our course discussions surrounded different ways of looking or thinking about church and relationships and it seemed as if this unexpected moment we found ourselves in globally was making room for something new. In 2021, in my last semester I was tired and wanted a break from all of the juggling of homeschool and rigorous study. I had a final course that was designed to wrap up everything about the Old and New Testament and applying it to the world today. The professor in this course held some theological views about Christ that became a stumbling block for me. I found myself trying to hold onto my beliefs against someone who couldn't reconcile the presence of evil in the world and questioned if the cross held any power at all. By now Trevor was begging me to throw in the towel and I almost did.

I still had no clear understanding of what was ahead of me after seminary or what I would do with a Bible degree. At this point all I wanted was to find an answer to this question that was growing louder within my spirit. The one question I had been asking and still had no answer to, how do we love one another despite our differences? Despite our theological views or understanding, how do we as the church love one another? Depending on what denomination you are a part of, your idea of what is right or wrong will vary significantly, so where do we stand together in agreement? Is there such a place to stand?

I always appreciate my husband's wisdom so I would ask him questions about certain doctrine or beliefs within the church and ask what side he landed on? Then I would give him the opposing view and ask what love would look like. Even his answers still sounded like judgement. I wasn't disagreeing because he was speaking what he believed to be truth but I wanted to know how he would speak truth in love to someone. Something in my heart was telling me there was another way. But neither of us had words for it. I continued to ask the question of love as I pressed through.

I was trying to find a new language around truth and love. When you love someone but want to speak truth to them what does it look like outside of relationship? What does that look like corporately as a body? Can you speak truth to someone that you do not love? It seemed to me that any truth spoken outside of an intimate relationship sounded like judgement or condemnation. There were many times in seminary I didn't feel safe enough to share how I felt if it opposed the majority of my classmates or professors because I feared judgment.

If others believed things that were the opposite of me I still wanted to do relationship with them. I'd look for their hearts and get to know them as friends. I'd value their stories and their ideas and the way they processed things. But when it came down to me sharing my core beliefs, I was afraid. It was much easier for me to keep my thoughts to myself than risk losing the respect and friendship of others. I had so many conflicting voices warring within me over which doctrines or theologies were the right ones or which politics or leaders were the right ones. Suddenly the meaning of the cross, the power of the cross faded into the backdrop of the noise around me and I was feeling further from the truth than where I started.

I had to finish one of my final papers for the course I was struggling with but I didn't know how to respond to the question about biblical interpretation and hermeneutics. But one morning I was cleaning and I went through some old boxes of memorabilia. As I rummaged through, I came across a hand written note from an old Starbucks regular of mine, Jan Spreeman. He was a great thinker and social studies teacher who I spent many mornings in deep conversations with. I did a quick search to see what he was up to and came across an obituary. It had been many years since we had last spoken and sadly I hadn't heard of his passing. I sat and read through his life and career and was reminded of his great wisdom and loving kindness. Even this hand written note found me at just the right time when

I needed it. His friendship was still blessing me even though he was no longer here.

I started to write my paper thinking about Jan's legacy. What was he remembered for? It reminded me of what the church was supposed to look like and the command that Jesus gave us to love one another. But the next words Christ spoke were the ones I was wrestling with. He said that this love will be the thing that will make everyone know that we are His. The thing that would set us apart – *if* that love could be found among us. (John 13:35)

Jessie DeCorsey
Course: Scripture and its Witness
Writing Assignment – Final Paper
Luther Seminary

When reading about Jan Spreeman and what his family, friends and community had to say about him was a great reminder of what it looks like to live in love. It was written that he believed everyone could make a difference in the world and the greatest gift he gave was love and compassion for all.[1] What is the legacy of the Christian church right now as it stands? I am almost haunted by the words in John's gospel when I think about them. "By this everyone will know that you are my disciples, if you have love for one another" I think the world is looking at the church and they see separation and division... "If we forsake our love for each other, we are also abandoning our love for Jesus. You cannot separate the two loves. We show our love

121

for God by loving each other, and we demonstrate that we love each other by loving God"[2,3]

My final theological summary was that we can't take one understanding of truth and apply it to all, but rather we can all come together as one and let the revelation start from relationship through love. In the end, what do we want to be remembered by? Our truth statements or our compassion and love for one another.

"I am the way, the truth and the life."

-John 14:6

In John, right after Jesus gives the new command to love one another He confuses the disciples by telling them about where He is going and how to get there. Both Peter and Thomas ask how they will know the way. He tells them that He is the way, and not only that, He is also the truth and the life. They are looking for a physical path to follow, but He is talking about the eternal path that is before them. So what does truth have to do with the way and the life? What is at stake if we get the truth wrong? Will that lead us to the wrong path?

Most of us today would agree that we think of the word truth as an indisputable fact. I was on jury duty once for a criminal case and saw firsthand the legal process of determining what the truth was. Everything was based on the evidence in the trial to inform us on what could be proven right or wrong. In English *truth* is derived from the word *troth*, it's a promise or something we would pledge ourselves to because we believe in it, we trust it. But looking deeper into the philosophy of truth, the ancient understanding had a much different concept surrounding its meaning. As a verb, the word for truth is an ongoing action and it's relational. It carries with it an understanding of faithfulness and loyalty.

In Hebrew, the word we often see as truth (*emet*) comes from the verb *aman*, which also has an understanding of something that is faithful and trustworthy from beginning, middle to end. The Greek however adds another layer to this concept. The word Jesus uses as truth is *aletheia*, meaning unconcealed or unforgetting.[4] The disciples think they don't know the way, so Jesus reveals that he is the unforgetting promise of Gods faithfulness to the world. And all who believe or entrust themselves to Him, have found the path and the life everlasting. It's not hidden or concealed, it is *aletheia*. "When Jesus says I am the truth, he is not saying I am the fact or I am a list of things for you to believe. In the Greek text he is saying "I am the unforgetting"; I am the incarnation of the unforgetting of God and His promises, I am literally God's unforgetting of you, in my birth and in my death and resurrection."[5]

As a seminarian, I had always been looking for the truth in the same way I was trying to get on the right path. I judged others based on whether I believed they were walking in truth. I also found myself being judged based on others beliefs. So often I hear the words that we as believers are commissioned to speak the truth in love. What that usually means is that someone has an idea of what truth is and feels they need to correct something, but quickly this becomes a substitution for love. When we are connected to each other relationally, truth follows because we can trust and have faith in each other and talk about our differences. So often we try to lead with our own understanding of truth over relationship. We hurt each other and let the walls around us get higher as we let division separate us because we cannot reconcile our truths. They determine the way we love.

So much of my life and my journey came from my heart's desire to find truth. I looked to everyone else to inform me of something that I already carried. It is His love and faithfulness that leads us into all understanding, this is the way and the life He was talking about. It's unforgetting and cannot be taken from us. "It is the act of holding a promise present in your mind and heart, letting that promise drive all that you do."[6] The Bible says that truth will set us free, and Jesus says, that truth is me and there is nothing that can separate us.

Jesus didn't come to show us how much we fall short of His glory or to judge us for how many times we get things wrong. It's a love story, not a trial. He came to reveal the fullness of His love for us so that we would know once and for all who we are. It's never been about getting it right or wrong. It has always been about love.

I crossed the finish line in the Spring of 2021 and spent the summer with my family after graduating. I enjoyed the sweetness of simplicity as my world slowed down and I loved the ones in front of me. I had gotten through one of the most grinding and challenging trials of my faith journey. I found myself burnt out on religion, on theology and trying to understand the church. I was thinking about the idea of how the Word became flesh to dwell among us, yet we are so focused on the Word itself that we lose all sense of His presence with us. We worship the word of God sometimes more than we worship the God of the word.

I was longing for a deep connection to a church. But a community that was centered around relationship and practiced a theology that started and ended with love. A church that used love as the agency of transformation to bless one another. Not a doctrine around judgement to shame others into the family of God. Author Alan Wright explains:

> When we bless, we partner with God to release the essence of His adopting love. Until we are blessed, we are like spiritual orphans looking for assurance. But when we are authentically blessed, it's like being adopted – we know for sure that we are loved. When we are blessed, we become secure. When we become secure, we soar.[7]

As God's family, blessing is our inheritance. We were made to soar. The body of Christ should look like a family that's united. Not divided. When we are divided we aren't soaring, we are falling. If Jesus is our truth, then it should unite us, not separate us from one another.

The striver in me was always afraid of failure and always afraid of making the wrong decision. I had gone to seminary thinking I was going to learn the right way to interpret the Bible, only to find out that there was and has never been one right way. You may find this challenging. I certainly have. But think about this, I can read a verse I have sat with a dozen times and find something new or challenging about it because I am changing and growing every day. My lens is different now than it was five years ago. How can we put all of our understanding of scripture on one person, one leader, or one denomination to interpret the Bible for all of us and give us the one right way of doing so? How are we finding ourselves connected to God's heart, the one who is truth, and letting our oneness with Him guide us into oneness and understanding with each other?

14

PERFECT WEAKNESS

"What does this world need? Gifted men and women, outwardly empowered? Or individuals who are broken, inwardly transformed?" [1]

-Gene Edwards

As we found ourselves in the midst of the pandemic and doing most of our connecting online I was able to do Immanuel Prayer and be part of a community of leaders and facilitators here in the Twin Cities area where this healing approach was becoming popular with church and ministry leaders and professional counselors. I also adapted it into my everyday life with friends and family who were going through challenging times while I continued my training with Stephanie and her team learning more about trauma and how we heal together in community. A group of us gathered together nearly a year reading through *The Other Half of Church* by Michel Hendricks and Jim Wilder. It breaks down a basic teaching of neurology about how the brain works and how we can experience transformation through community based attachment.

It centers on how much we need joy and how we were created to be a part of communities that are happy to be with us. "Joy is a right-brain dominant emotion requiring face to face interactions."[2] Our left eye gives information to the right side of our brain on how to feel. One of the first lessons I learned at our training was the importance of left eye to left eye contact. It's something I use daily in my interactions, especially at home with my family. It is a simple exercise I do with others to illustrate the importance of spending time with God and others *face to face*.

Let's say I'm near my husband and I tell him how much I appreciate him and what he means to me but we are not looking at each other. He will *hear* the words I'm saying and they will be very affirming. If I transition and sit directly across from him and we are facing one another, I look into his eyes and I tell him I love him and appreciate him; our brains have just synchronized and we are sharing a mutual mind state where we *experience* being loved.[3] Wilder often says our brain's greatest desire is to be the sparkle in someone's eye. Words that are spoken with a face that is happy to be with us makes us experience what it is to be loved, seen and known. When I speak identity or love over my children I make sure we connect through our eyes so that we can connect through our hearts.

When we had our first child, I had read in all of the developmental books that said by week five he should be able to look at me and smile because facial recognition would have developed. At five weeks to the day the sun was rising and our son was laying in my arms looking up at me. He looked right into my eyes and smiled the biggest smile. I can still see it perfectly. Up until that moment he had smiled but never in a communicative way. This smile, before he had words to tell me how he felt, told me that He knew and loved me. The love I felt in that moment is hard to wrap words around. It was the moment I knew our love was a mutual mind moment. Jesus intends His church to function as a family that is bonded together with joyful attachments of love.[4] Attachment love or bonding together happens when we sit face to face with each other and our experiences and memories shape our identities and build our character. This is what love looks and feels like in community and when it's absent in our time together and our time with God, we don't see the transformation we desire. We so often center our gatherings together on teaching and believe that will change our hearts but it's missing the source of oneness and connectedness that can only be found as we turn towards each other. We were designed to be in safe communities where people are happy to be with us when we have it all together and when we are falling apart.

My life in the church had connection until everything fell apart. I didn't know how to share my hopelessness, my pain or the depression I was suffering. As Christians I think we avoid sharing our pain because it makes people uncomfortable or we feel uncomfortable being vulnerable with others for fear of judgment. It was in my isolation in that painful season when I realized I needed to have deeper meaningful experiences in community. "Loosely connected communities and performance-based churches avoid pain by limiting attachment to each other, but they miss out on the extravagant family love of God."[5] In my experience of walking with people through their suffering, I found more joy in those connections through pain than I was experiencing anywhere else. What would it take to become a people that do not shy away from pain and discomfort? "Our brains were designed to respond to group identity in order to help us act like 'our people.'"[6] I was reading this fresh out of Seminary and finding a lot of common language around some of my experiences and experiences of others who I was doing ministry with. I had a lot of questions around what a church would look like if we gathered together with relationship being our primary group identity verses our belief statement to define who we are as a people.

The book study was compelling because it explained a lot of the dilemma where the church has become less relation based and more like a classroom. The chapter that resonated with me the most after years of studying the church talked about the full-brained pastor. It defined them as:

> The relational pastor intentionally stays small. People are not impressed by this pastor, except by his humility and maturity...The pastor is but one of many people in a community where all faithfully complete the assignments Jesus gave them.

> Pastors and other leaders stay small and act like trainers
> – laser focused on creating a relational environment that
> foster transformation.[7]

In my own journey this is something that became personal for me because of my own experience elevating leaders and pastors. As though they were the only ones that had the full knowledge of who God was and if I wanted to be closer to God then I had to follow them.

Prior to starting my courses in seminary we were required to take a boundaries course. They talked about how hard it is as a Christian public leader to have friendships within and out of the church because of the social hierarchies that will always be present. They warned, as soon as people know you have attended seminary you will be looked at and upheld with expectations. People will now be watching you; the world will be watching you as you are a representative of the Christian faith. The reality is, and not many talk about it, pastors and ministry leaders are some of the loneliest people within the church because of the pressure and weight they carry to be a model of Christ. I had great conversations with some of my peers who were pastoring churches for years and how nice it was to be in a classroom with others pastors and let themselves let loose a little. In our churches today, we don't allow our leaders off the podium. We want them to be the model of perfection. If they show the slightest error we judge them and their families as if they aren't people with problems like the rest of us. I have great respect for the leaders and pastors of the church today because I have seen firsthand the price they have paid and the sacrifices they have made. The rejection and betrayals they have endured as they give all of themselves to their communities. Most are often lacking time for their own healing and transformation but have to be responsible for an entire community and meeting the demands and needs of everyone around them. It's no wonder we see our leaders burn out and fall so often.

The very idea of what Wilder and his colleagues were presenting was upsetting because it was hard to imagine a church that is willing to be less classroom and platform driven. Why? Because we have had no other model. This just added more fuel to the fire I had post-graduation. Because I was experiencing radical transformation in myself and all who I was ministering to, I wanted to find a community and leaders that were focused on the transformation of their people. Because for me, that was the only way I was able to know God's love. What God showed me was that His desire first and foremost is our hearts. Without the inner healing I was missing the most important part of my relationship with Him. Helping others find their connection to Him became my priority over finding the right denomination. This kind of love and attachment cannot be replaced with facts and knowledge –right or wrong.

When we gathered in our small group to discuss this very thing, all of us struggled to imagine what this meant and how to build something like this within our own groups or communities that we were a part of. A body of believers that do not shy away from brokenness but push towards it for healing, who are attached to the vine and bearing fruit that brings forth the transformative powers of love. Not a perfect people, but a people who are being perfected in weakness. Who come together to discuss both the beauty and challenges of scripture and don't contend to know it all. There was no way I could have foreseen the set up that God had in store for me that was just around the corner, but across the world.

15

THE POWER OF PRESENCE

In the fall our youngest started kindergarten and all of our children were back in school. It was a strange new place and a new pace of life. During the pandemic I had laid down the ministries I was a part of to focus on school and our family's needs at the time. I was spending a lot of time with the Lord reflecting on the past few years of seminary. I was recalling how He told me it was going to be something He did within me, but I was struggling to understand what that meant. I suppose it was because of the weariness I was feeling and I was counting the cost. Was it worth it? God could you show me it was worth it. By now I didn't feel anything in me but frustration.

I woke up on October 4th, 2021 with the word emulsifier chiming in my head. The last time this had happened it was the word seminary and that was the catalyst of a long journey I was still processing. I was curious to know what it meant. I had to look up the definition because it wasn't a word I was familiar with. An emulsifier is a sort of bonding agent that takes two liquids that cannot come together like oil and water and allows them to become one. What an interesting concept. What would it take to bind the church together? What is that bonding agent that could take two opposing sides and bring them into unity? The Lord showed me how prior to seminary I had tried to attach myself to a single theology, but He used my inability to do so to give me His heart for His people over a religion. This was the *something in me* He had spoken about and love was the emulsifying agency of His people.

A few years prior, my mother forwarded me an email that had an encouraging word in it for the season I was in. I had been following the ministry that it came from for a while now and felt nudged to check out a few of their online courses. As I was scanning through their content, someone came on a video I was watching and began to speak life into all the weariness I was carrying.

His name was Matt Beckenham from Sydney, Australia where he and his wife Trish were pastoring a church. He shared his heart for others knowing the love of the Father and something in the way he spoke about this kind of love was different than any kind of preaching or teaching I had come across.

I went through several more videos to learn about his church and what they had to say. Time and time again he was bringing everything back to simple yet profound concepts of love. He was saying love is measured by presence, without presence love is just a word. I had been searching and longing to understand how we love. It was the one question that I had been measuring everything I knew against but could not come to an understanding of what love looked like in a community of believers - especially ones that are divided. How do we come together through attachment in joy and suffering? What does a relationally based church look like? It had seemed too complicated to sort out but Beckenham introduced me to this way of understanding love inseparable from presence. In fact he introduced me to an entirely new vocabulary about love of which I could not have put a single word down on these pages if it wasn't for these revelations. I didn't have the vocabulary until our paths crossed and God was able to knit everything together in a beautiful tapestry.

Within a matter of weeks of listening to a variety of teachings I was undone. How had we missed this in the church? How did I miss this in my own life? How did we not realize that we can say we love one another, but if we are not present with each other, we do not have love? I welcomed the challenge of some of the things he was presenting. It wasn't based on my works, it wasn't based on what I could do for others, and it wasn't based on knowledge, strategy, having the right thing to say or fixing people. It was simple - almost too simple. It was being present with the one in front of me. Listening to the heart of the one in front of me. Creating safety for the one in front of me. This is where love casts out all fear and binds up all wounds. Love through presence has the power to restore and redeem our identities and let us encounter the love of the Father in ways we will never be the same again. When love is present, He is present. Beckenham was saying that this was something we can easily do in the church. This took the idea of how our brains are seeking joyful connection through attachment and community and gave it wings to soar. This was the model I was looking for.

Every teaching Beckenham did, no matter the topic, came back to the indisputable theology surrounding love and relationship, "Jesus didn't need an army to change the world, He needed a bunch of friends that would walk with him. He didn't need huge strategies or five-year plans."[1] He illustrated the way Christ chose to be present with people time and time again throughout the scriptures and tied it back to our original design in the Garden of Eden where God walked with those He loved. We were never supposed to understand who God is through a theology first; we were supposed to gain an understanding of God through relationship so understanding can flow from there. The same way we come to understand one another when we are present with each other. I couldn't tell you what being a mom was like until I became a mother and experienced that kind of love. I couldn't tell you what kind of selfless love my husband has given me throughout our lives together if I hadn't experienced it daily. I could never teach about it or help others understand it if it wasn't something I had encountered.

It's always been our hearts that God desires above all else. There is no love without presence and truth and revelation will flow from the power of love that will manifest when we come together. There is no substitute and it cannot be taught, it must be lived and experienced. This is the place where transformation occurs. Why is this important? Because Christ called us to love others as we love ourselves. For many of us, we need help understanding what that looks like. What if it is as simple as being present?

The one thing God commanded above all else is the very thing we have minimized and spent little time investing in, love and presence. For me the two words have now become one in the same. For so long I believe the body of Christ has separated these two components by building the church on theologies which has and will always lead to division. When we let division replace presence we no longer have love. We have two liquids that cannot come together, Oil and water. Presence is the absence of judgement and an invitation to love each other despite our circumstances, beliefs, failures or shortcomings.

This was everything that Wilder and colleagues explained neurologically in the way we were created to be relational first and form attachment to God and in community. What Beckenham was modeling was in perfect alignment to their concept of the full-brained pastor too. Until now, everything I had read remained on the pages as something too complex to know how to build and start in community. Beckenham suggested, "To learn to see someone as God sees them is an act of love that is as normal as breathing."[2] Seeing someone required being present with them. We cannot see someone as God sees them without relationship and intimacy the same way we cannot bypass experiencing God by hearing about Him. It has to be encountered. In the Bible Job suffered and was left alone in his pain. He lost everything, and was misunderstood by all who knew and loved Him. The theology of the day didn't fit with his circumstances. He was the most blameless and upright man on earth yet he felt he was being punished. This didn't fit the paradigm of the day. Only sin was punishable. He didn't see or understand where God was present in all of this. Then Job encountered God through the whirlwind and everything changed. I had only heard about you before, but now my eyes have seen you. (Job 42:5) This shows us the power of presence. Ellen Davis says, "It is not only his theology that is renewed; it is his whole mind."[3] It wasn't the friends who falsely accused Job, although I always feel bad for the friends because they truly were working with the religious beliefs that they all knew and lived from. They thought they were going to help fix Job's circumstances but they missed what Job needed the most. People who were able to be in the depths of his despair without judgement, the ministry of presence.

Beckenham redefined the understanding of love as more than a word, it's an encounter of presence that has the power to deliver, heal, set free and redeem. This is how we pioneer a new standard for the church by returning it to the original design. In his book *Eden's Blueprint* he speaks about the Fathers heart as a place that is safe, transforming and loving.

> These are often the last words that people use to describe churches these days. Churches have become known more for judgement, or lack of judgement, rather than for love. I think this is a natural flow-on effect from generations of being told what God has said rather than hearing what God has said, and it needs to change.[4]

Truth was never meant to lead us to love. Love was always meant to lead us into truth - the unforgetting faithfulness of God.

Matt and Trish Beckenham are both passionate about teaching others to hear and see God for themselves and release people into the fullness of their identities. They are pioneering an international community where they see transformation move freely as people gather and their voices are heard. And it's not about valuing one voice over the other. Restoration is the fruit of the relationships that are formed through the love that is encountered. This, I believe, is the essence of church we see in the book of Acts and the heart of the Father in our midst. I believe the theology of presence that Beckenham teaches is the most potent and powerful doctrine of our day. It has the ability to change the history of the church and the world if people could experience what it's like to come together relationally and not religiously.

16

GETTING IT RIGHT

There is a saying we read over and over again in the Old Testament that talks about staying on the straight path. After Moses died the Lord spoke to Joshua and promised to always be with him wherever he would go. However, He cautioned him to obey the laws of Moses and to not turn to the left hand or to the right. (Josh 1:7) In other places it can mean more of a directional saying where someone will seek permission to travel through the land. They make an agreement to stay on the path and not go to the left hand or the right. In ancient Israel this saying would have the understanding that the correct path was the straight one. The one that didn't go to the left or right. It was the moral way. It was the narrow way, where one was not led astray through sin, temptation or disobedience. This was the path that I longed to stay on. My earliest introduction to God was rooted in fear and legalism, following a set of laws or rules. This embedded itself into my attachment to religion to keep me on the narrow path, which would lead me to the narrow gate so that I could enter it and find salvation.

I thought to have God's favor, for him to use me, to love me and redeem me required a life that looked like the straight path. But as I started layering this old belief system to the one that I was learning, I came to the realization that the narrow path was Him. He was less concerned about me getting it right than He was about walking it out with me. Beckenham writes, "the day Jesus was born was the day the gate to the narrow path was thrown open, never to be closed again. It may be controversial but I believe that the wide road is religion and the narrow path is our personal relationship with God and others."[1] Is it that controversial though? A quick Google search yields the results that there are approximately 40,000 different Christian denominations.[2] That is a broad road with many different concepts of how to find the narrow gate. Consequently, I had associated the gate with religion not a relationship – no wonder I failed to find the right theology despite my great efforts. The psalmist writes, the gates lead to the presence of the Lord, and the godly enter there. (Psa 118:20) Jesus even calls Himself the gate in the gospel of John. Yet, I had confused presence with performance and Christ with a theology.

As I tried to find my identity in a religion it was as though I was standing on a pathway heading in the direction I believed to be the narrow gate. As I did this I followed the voices of others calling, "come this way it's over here." As I stood with them it wouldn't be too long before I heard another voice calling, "No you're standing on the wrong path it's over here." So I would quickly join that voice and back and forth I journeyed seeking the straight path. What I wasn't aware of, was that Christ was with me and with everyone around me saying, "I am the path. Seek me." When I encountered His presence all of the voices around me disappeared and I found myself with Him. I found my identity and soon I was no longer concerned on what path others were on. I just wanted them to see who was with them on their path so that they could find themselves as well. There were two things that kept me from being able to find the narrow path that was my personal relationship with Christ; A false identity and getting stuck trying to figure out the right thing to do.

Understanding trauma and the ways that we try to avoid pain, helped reveal the places in my life that I had a distorted understanding of who I was and who God was. I was living my life in fear of pain and trying to avoid it at all costs. "When we are controlled by fear we will rarely be able to see or live in the fullness that Jesus came to lead us into."[3] Fear may lead us to the left or right and off the path of presence with Him. Pain will make us forget who we are.

This last spring I was at my son's baseball game and the other team had a really strong pitcher that threw hard and fast. In previous games our team had confidence rising to the plate and swinging hard. This time, each player got up to bat and wouldn't take a single pitch. They were afraid of getting hit by a pitch at such a high speed. Many of them had experienced this before in practice, or watched others get hurt by a rogue throw that would land in the chest or arm. If they were to get hit by a ball at this speed there would be some kind of injury. Their brains were telling them this would be something that would cause great pain so it was in their best interest to not get closer to the plate. They were not able to be themselves because pain was directing their path.

They each initially went up to the plate with a deep desire to hit a homerun. But the part of their brain that wanted to avoid pain was overriding their systems as a means of protection. This often happens without our knowing or our permission. I had no idea until the Lord showed me that the unhealed pain I had from my childhood was doing the same thing for me today as a grown woman.

> Our brains will carefully record the impact of trauma with intense emotional signals that will replay themselves in our brains intrusively. The impact of traumas throughout our lives combined with very few memories of being loved by God will create weakness.[4]

Trauma can be defined as something bad that happened or the absence of something good that we didn't receive. Both require presence from God and enduring love relationships to process and heal the pain of these intense emotional signals that can trigger us and make us forget who we are.[5]

My Identity was restored when I spent time with Jesus and encountered His love for me. The more time I spent with Him the more memories I made and the more transformation came. I went from believing I was unworthy of His love, to knowing His love for me was nothing I had to earn or achieve. I was loved simply because I am His daughter. When we try to avoid looking at our pain, we miss the opportunity to complete the process of healing we need. The more time I spent in my weakness with Him, the more completed I became.

In the Bible Paul asks Jesus to take away a thorn in his flesh. Christ responds that His grace was sufficient and His power was perfected in weakness. When we read the verse about perfect love casting out fear we see another use of the word perfect. Why did the authors add the word perfect when talking about the power of Christ or the love of Christ? I usually associate the word perfect with flawlessness or being strong with no weakness and without blemish. The root word *telos* found in the Greek for *perfect* or *perfected* means something closer to completed, finished, or the necessary process for reaching the end.[6] We hear the root word *telos* again when Christ calls out Tetelestai on the cross, *"It is finished."* (John 19:30) It was Christ's perfect love that sent him to the cross and God's love for us that gave His one and only Son. In both English and Hebrew the original meaning of perfect means something closer to wholeness and integrity.

With His death, the curtains were torn in the holy of holies and we were invited to encounter the very presence of God.[7] The bible says God is love. When we encounter love we are perfected, completed and made whole. We try to create an understanding of what the cross did for us. There are many theories on atonement or the reason Christ died through sacrifice. We often associate the message of the cross as a ransom or payment for our sin verses a restoration of relationship. The word atonement means at one or condition of being at one (with

147

others). The Hebrew word for sacrifice or offering is *Korban*, but it has a root word associated with an intimate understanding of coming close or drawing near (to God).[8] Being perfected in Christ is knowing why He died for us. We were created for relationship with Him and each other. Unhealed pain can turn us away from who we are, but resolving pain through Christ will make us one with Him – reconciled. The meaning of reconciliation is about restoring harmony and perhaps the idea of perfection has always been about restoring harmony between ourselves and God.

If we return to the story of Job for a moment, we see a man who is in unimaginable pain and suffering but through presence and encounter is transformed. Davis writes,

> From this book above all others in scripture we learn that the person in pain is a theologian of unique authority. The sufferer who keeps looking for God has, in the end, privileged knowledge. The one who complains to God, pleads with God, rails at God, does not let God off the hook for a minute – she is at last admitted to a mystery. She passes through a door that only pain will open, and is thus qualified to speak of God in a way that others, whom we generally call more fortunate, cannot speak.[9]

I meet with many Christians who are afraid to rail at God or plead with God because they think that is a sign of weakness or even sinful. But holding onto Him is also knowing that He is first and foremost holding onto us. He is not separate from our pain or weakness; He is holding it with us indivisible.

During that same baseball game I spoke about earlier, our youngest daughter was running towards me and accidentally ran into a table nearby. I opened my arms to her as the pain set in and the tears started to flow. I picked her up and watched as she tried to be strong. I couldn't stop her from the pain she was feeling but in that moment we shared in it together as I held her tightly through it. Her pain was also my pain and how much greater does Christ in us experience our pain as we are one with Him.

Jesus revealed to me in that moment with my daughter, this is what He was doing in me as well. It wasn't about avoiding pain or suppressing it or being strong enough to rise above it. It was allowing the pain to process and be felt with Him. So often I get discouraged by my weakness. I want to be stronger and have more faith like others who seem to endure hardship and disappointment much better than I. I thought for the longest time that my love for Him was measured by the amount of faith I had. Faith was a result of my strength to trust him. But He's shown me that faith isn't measured by strength. Faith is the fruit of being attached to the vine. Faith is the result of love and relationship. It's not determined by the strength I can generate on my own, faith generates itself as a result of my relationship to Him - my attachment to Him. In the same way, we struggle when we try to navigate our circumstances alone. When we try to know the right thing to do without seeking the Kingdom first.

What if God never intended for us to have all the knowledge needed to know the right thing to do? What if that knowledge is only something that, like faith, comes from being attached to the vine? What if when we strive to choose the right path in our lives, finances, careers, relationships, calling etc. it is the same as walking the broad road? We get so caught up in our circumstances trying to make the right decision without having the full picture. Only God has the whole view, so why do we carry the weight of navigating it without him? There are times that we think we are doing something right and good when we are actually doing or thinking the wrong thing.[10] We may think that a blessing is a curse when actually it was the very thing that God used to bring a blessing. We may judge something that someone does to us as bad, but it was the path that led to healing and wholeness. We may think a closed door is the end of a dream and we are finished but God had a bigger dream behind another door that we hadn't imagined. We may judge a person by their actions and call them a Saul but God was using that Saul to create a David, both anointed by God. In the end who has the authority to make the final judgment?

I spend a lot of time praying with people who are full of anxiety and depression because they are afraid to make the wrong decision for their lives. I often hear them say, "I don't know what God wants me to do." In my own experience I've struggled time and time again thinking I might screw up God's plans for me, I might miss an opportunity out of fear or disobedience. Or sometimes if I am waiting on the Lord for something I thought He promised, I'll wonder if He really said that. Especially when my circumstances aren't changing and I don't see the fulfillment of that promise. When I can't trust my own discernment I stop trusting Him. I will question God's timing and start making decisions out of fear that I've missed out. Or I'll fall back into old patterns of wondering if He really loves me. All of this as a result of trying to figure out the right thing to do. Striving in my own effort to make the best decision believing it to be the straight path but finding myself on the broad road that steers me to the left hand or the right.

If we go back to where my story began, I was challenged by what Jesus said to my friend, "It's not about getting it right, it's about walking it out with me," I felt an invitation from Him to understand His heart once again. I started to imagine what a life apart from getting it right could look like. What kind of invitation was on the table and what was at stake if I didn't have to worry about getting things wrong all the time? And most importantly, what does walking it out with Jesus look like?

When the religious leaders were conspiring against Christ for not doing the right thing, like healing on the Sabbath, Jesus said that He could do nothing by Himself, unless He saw the Father doing it. (John 5:19) Even Jesus didn't take it upon Himself for having to know if what He was doing was right or wrong. His straight and narrow path was doing it with His Father. Later in John, Jesus explained to His disciples that He was doing what the Father commands *so that* the world may know that He loves the Father. (John 14:31). When we hear the word command it sounds very un-relational. The words love and command do not seem to fit together. If we break down the word for command in the

Greek we see *entellomai*. This takes us back to the root word *telos* where something is working towards the end objective. It is a movement of completion of instruction through *tellomai* or enjoining.[11] Jesus looked to His Father to *join together*. The will of the Father came to Christ through being present together. Knowing the right thing to do came through presence for the sake of love. Jesus knew who He was because He remained in the Father. He didn't let fear or pain steal His identity. He didn't look to His own strength to bring anything to completion, but joined together with His Father's heart - so that the world would know love.

Jesus also invites us to join together in the same way, "love one another: just as I have loved you, you also are to love one another. By this all people will know that you are my disciples, *if* you have love for one another." (John 13:34-35, ESV) We should never underestimate the power of love, for love is the very thing that creates life and conquers death. Love casts out all fear and isn't worried about a theology or getting it right. Our identity is not based on our knowledge of God, it's completed in Him. The word identity comes from the Latin word *idem* meaning *the same*.[12] I am yours and you are mine were the words that changed my life. They gave birth to an identity, a sameness that I hadn't known was the very essence of who I was. The very one who created heaven and earth calls me His and there is nothing that can separate His love from me. Even when I strayed off path time and time again, was I ever lost? Was I ever alone? Love knows no limits and knows no boundaries and Christ will go to the ends of the earth for you and me.

We encounter His presence when we love as He has loved us. It doesn't matter which path you have taken or which path you are on now – He wants you to know that He is with you. He has always been with you. If you need help knowing which way to go look to Him, you may find that you are exactly where you are meant to be.

EPILOGUE
AN IMMANUEL PRAYER

I leave you, the reader, with this final word. It is my prayer that through my own journey with Immanuel, *God with us*, you will be able to see Him within your own story. Immanuel prayer is something that allows me to freely explore the heart of God in ways that I can better understand Him. This creative piece I'm sharing with you captures some of the conversations we often have as I imagine what it means to *walk with Him* through the joys and challenges in this world.

A Love Story

I was up in the morning before the rest of my household began to stir. I walked quietly to my favorite outdoor seat to enjoy the smooth taste of my morning coffee. With a pen and journal in hand, I sat down and settled into my blue cushioned chair while the birds sang their morning songs. It was my favorite time of day to meet with Immanuel.

Hands folded under my chin I prayed, "Where would you like to meet with me today my Lord?"

Before my words had finished a familiar memory came to mind. It was Collaroy. A beautiful beachy place I loved to revisit often. I melted into my chair and remembered the feel of the sand beneath my feet and the cool ocean breeze on my face. Suddenly I could sense Jesus sitting beside me in the chair.

"Do you remember the seaglass on the shoreline and how much had washed up in a cluster at your feet?"

"Yes my Lord. More than I had ever laid my eyes on before. I didn't have enough pockets to contain that much treasure!"

He laughed as He watched me smiling from ear to ear in thought of the tumbled remnants that littered the shoreline.

"Most would consider this trash, but not you. You find beauty in the broken pieces. Do you know why that is?"

I thought about it for a moment, "Each piece is unique and carries with it a story." I continued after another pause, "I like to imagine whose hands made this long ago and what it was created for. Whenever I pick it up I feel like I'm holding onto a journey."

He nodded as if He had already known why I loved the seaglass but delighted in hearing me express it nonetheless.

"There's something beautiful about each one. And I love the new creation they become when they are all displayed together."

I started writing quickly and recorded the conversation we were sharing. I did this every time we met so I could always remember His words and our time together. Never wanting to forget a single memory we made.

He watched me intently as I scribbled away.

"Is there anything else you want to share with me today Lord?" I asked before I looked up from my journal.

"Yes. There is. In fact there are a few things I'd like to share with you today."

My eyes widened with anticipation. I loved it when He said this to me. I knew I was in for a great adventure.

"Do you remember that pool in Collaroy on the beach next to the ocean?" He asked.

I closed my eyes and recalled the times I walked past the pool He was talking about.

"Yes Lord. I remember. I can see families nearby with little children walking into the shallows. What is it you wanted to show me about this?"

He looked me in the eyes, "Something, but first, you have been wrestling with some big questions about me this week and I would like to show you something of my heart today."

"Yes I have." I nodded in agreement. "Are you ready?"

"Ask away." He said while folding His hands in His lap and settling into the chair we were sharing.

"I can't seem to prove one way or another how much you know about our future before it happens. I can see so many times in my life where you put things in my path that you could have only done had you known which path I would take. I can also see many stories in scripture where you talk about things to come. Words that tell me you have the ability to know and see all that ever has been, is and will come to be."

He took a deep breath and looked at my furred brows as I continued on.

"There have been times in my life where you came for me when I was on a path of destruction and lifted me out of the darkness I was in. Even when I didn't ask you for help, you rescued me. You stopped me from making choices that were hurting others or hurting myself. But there have also been times you let me stumble and fall and you didn't intervene. In those moments I felt alone and unloved by you."

I held my breath for a minute as I was afraid to continue. "Other times you led me to places or brought me to people." I stopped for a few seconds as I swallowed back my tears. This wound was all too real and too fresh to not be felt.

I started again. "Other times you led me to places or brought people into my life who I thought you had called me to. I followed your voice diligently and there I met the most hurt I had ever experienced. I only went because I listened to you. Had I said no, I would have been better off."

Tears now streamed down my face. "Did you know those things would happen when you called me?"

I looked over to see tears falling down His face too.

"Yes." He said as He looked towards the sky that was now changing colors with the rising sun.

"How can you do that? If you knew, why didn't you stop it? I don't understand."

I closed my eyes and lowered my head as the tears pooled in my lap.

"This is why it's so hard for me to trust you. It doesn't make sense. If you are a good father, why do you let these things happen the way they do?"

He said nothing as I continued on. "How can I trust anything you say to me? Or any promise you've given or any place you're asking me to go? Why should I put my trust in you if you're not going to protect me? Or stop me from making the wrong decisions or be led astray? Or stop others from hurting me? Or let things happen to the people I love?"

He waited until my words were dried up as the earth and grass around us. The soil hadn't seen rain for months and everything was supposed to be green but instead looked parched and lifeless.

"Can I show you something now that I wanted to share with you? He asked with a soft voice that calmed my spirit and returned my gaze to His.

"Yes, my Lord."

"Close your eyes, if you will, and tell me what you see."

I let my eyelids fall together, "I see Collaroy again but this time I see a dark storm over the water. It's coming fast and I see lightning and hear thunder exploding over crashing waves." My face grew tense. "Lord a storm? Is there something bad coming that I should be worried about?"

"This storm is not bad for a thirsty ground is it? Storms like this one carry my provision. This storm carries the prayers of my creation and my people who are dependent on this rain. Each thunderclap is awakening the hardened ground to make way for the rain that will soften and bring healing and new life. Listen and you'll hear the voice of my spirit roaring over my creation." He looked again deeply into my eyes as I was soaking in His words. He knew I was weighing them out with my own life and experiences.

"Yes. I can hear and see what you're saying. It's as if you're in every drop of rain. And it's almost like I can see the prayers of every person carried in each one as well. But my Lord, storms can also be menacing and destructive. They can take life. A storm can steal someone's dreams and hopes by damaging their livelihood and they can shipwreck people or toss them out to sea."

"This is true. All you say is true. But they can also reveal the lies you believe and the truths you need."

These words were familiar to me from the author Susie Larson. Something I had long believed to be true for it was a powerful word I came across in a season of my life that I had been shipwrecked.

"Those storms were the menacing kind. Destructive."

I thought a little harder. "But they did reveal the lies I had believed and the truths I did need. They led me to you. They led me to your love in a way that the lies I was believing, before the storm, had kept me from knowing you and your heart."

"But those lies were never able to keep me from knowing you," He said with a smile as we both wiped the tears from our eyes and dried off our wet cheeks.

I was now thinking of how hard my heart had been in those years before the storm. How I was living my life lost, but the storms and the pain I endured led me to His love in ways I had never imagined were possible. Like the earth that breaks open for new life to spring up after a season of plentiful rain.

160

"How many prayers do you think were answered in those drops of rain from the storms you weathered?" He spoke as if He was responding directly to my thoughts.

"What about the prayers of people who were hurting, broken and lost. That felt alone in their suffering but found their way to you where they received healing when you shared in their pain. A place others dared not go with them for they were in the depths of their hurt, but you had swam in the deep places and were not afraid to meet with them there. It was there, many of them met me through your love, some for the first time."

Jesus was tearing up again as He looked upon my face which was fixed on the bottom of my empty coffee cup.

I spoke after a while, "Even now I can see the faces of so many that showed up on my doorstep during those years. They had no idea when they came what I had walked through, but somehow they continued to find me. One after another. And through our shared suffering, the most exquisite healing happened. And that was when I encountered the power of your love and the way it transforms, heals and redeems all things. Even the most broken things."

"So you see that it is not easy to judge the storms in your life as good or bad?" Jesus added.

"Impossible." I sighed. "But either way they leave their mark. And we are never the same again, my Lord."

"No my daughter, you are never the same again. Close your eyes once more and tell me what you see now."

I set my coffee down and picked up my pen so I could continue to write. "I see all the broken discarded glass lost at sea."

"Not all broken things are lost." He interjected as I wrote, and when I heard these words my pen stopped in my hand.

"I see each of their journeys on the seafloor and the way they were tumbled and refined. And now I see them washing to shore at my feet and they are radiant with their colors and shapes. They reflect the light and shine like diamonds, each one unique and wonderful."

"Anything else?" He asked.

"I can see your perfect timing for when I came upon them, it wasn't anything I had orchestrated, but it was your hand that placed them there at the exact right moment knowing I had eyes for such treasures." Joy was now spread across my face as I stood in this moment with Him. "I think they are more beautiful now than they were when they were whole, before they were broken."

"Let me ask you another question this morning. Do you think my plans include breaking or destroying my creation and the ones I have loved and called by name?"

"Is this a trick question Lord?" I replied as I scrunched up my nose.

"No. This is a question as old as time." He spoke quietly now.

"If I must answer, then yes. It does seem to me that this is all your doing. If you're telling me you see and know all things before they come to be, and you are all powerful, then it must be your doing. But that means you cannot be an all loving God because a loving father would not be able to stand by and watch us be destroyed by others or ourselves."

Silence stood between us again. This time we both allowed it for a few minutes as we watched the trees moving in the gentle breeze that was now stirring around us.

"I can't do this. I can't figure you out. You're too complicated," I said with honesty.

"Go back to the moment where we started today at the pool and tell me what you notice about a little girl holding her father's hand," He said and waited for me to imagine myself back in Collaroy.

"I see a father and a little girl with curly hair. She must be two or three years old. He is leading her to the water's edge in the shallow and letting go of her hand as she splashes around the water. I can feel the love he has for his daughter as he watches her explore."

I was concentrating now on what I saw next and stopped speaking. My face tightened and I felt as though I was having a bad dream.

Finally I spoke, "I saw the father, he got distracted by another child they were with. He walked away from his little girl to tend to his other child. When he left, she followed at first, but then walked out of the shallow end where he had left her. She found her way to the edge of the wall where waves and strong currents were swirling out of control with jagged rocks beneath them. She was mesmerized by their movement and leaned over the edge to see further. In no time at all she lost her footing and began to topple into the water." I paused before I continued.

"I yelled to the father to save her. He looked at his helpless daughter and didn't move. I yelled for him to hurry but he yelled back to me, '*This was her choice*.' I ran to the edge but I was too late. She was nowhere to be seen."

"Jessie, do you think a father would ever do this? Is there any father who loves his daughter that would stand by and watch her be thrown into the crushing waves?"

"NO! I can't imagine any father who would stand by and be unmoved like this. Why are you showing me this?"

"Do you know how much I love you? Do you know that there is no place in the world that you could go that I wouldn't be with you? That there is no choice you could ever make that would keep me from moving towards you. Why is it that you think I would leave you alone and abandon you when you need me most?"

I fired back, "Because! If you knew this kind of thing was going to happen, which by the way, horrible things like this do happen all the time, then this is how I see you – unmoved and unshaken. You are just like that father who stood by and did nothing!"

"I am many things, but I am not him. But this is the lie you believe about me."

I took a deep breath and held it before saying, "I know Lord. My heart knows this to be true but my head tells me another story. Show me the truth; give me your eyes to see."

Jesus took my hand and held it tightly as I went back into my mind by the ocean's edge. This time, He was standing next to me at Collaroy and to my surprise, next to the little girl as she wandered away from her father. Jesus was holding her tiny hand the whole time, as she walked to the edge and started to fall towards the water. He held tightly to her so she didn't move. Jesus then drew the father's attention to what was unfolding and as he saw what was happening he yelled and ran to her side and scooped her into his loving arms.

"Love cannot and will not ever be unmoved in the face of fear, pain or darkness. Watch once more." He spoke softly.

This time I saw myself in the pool with my own children. While they were enjoying a swim my youngest got out of the pool and walked over to where the little girl had been and tiptoed on the edge near the waves that appeared to grow in size each time we revisited this scene.

"Would you, as her mother, be able to stand by and watch her fall?"

I felt this deep in my heart. "No, my Lord, I could never stand by and watch this without doing anything."

"Because you are a good mother. Because love cannot stand by and watch loved ones be destroyed and do nothing about it. What would you do if she did fall in the water right now?"

"Lord, I would jump in the water after her. I would never stop until I found her. I would give my life to save hers."

"Ahh my beautiful daughter. Now you speak the truth. This is what love does."

My eyes were leaking again as I was no longer in Collaroy. I was at Calvary at the foot of the cross. Looking up I saw Jesus with crimson flowing from His body. I wept at the sight of my savior on the cross hanging lifeless.

"Why are you crying?" A familiar voice filled my ears. I had forgotten Jesus was still holding tightly to my hand in my chair.

"You loved us this much. That you died so that we could know there is no place you wouldn't go to save us. That we have never and will never be alone in this world, no matter what darkness we may face, no matter what decisions we may make."

"Now you are seeing my heart. This is who *I Am*."

"So why does it have to hurt so much? Why does there have to be so much pain in the world? Why must we be so broken?"

"Now that you see how love cannot ever be unmoved by darkness, I need you to hold onto that; for it is one thing that will never change. Next I want to show you something about pain."

We both were now looking at each other again as we sat in my yard. The sun was almost all the way up and the birds' songs were getting quieter as the daylight grew.

"When pain is present it feels like love was absent. But here is something I want you to remember. I am love. And I am never absent. But sometimes you cannot see where love was present in pain. But I was always there, and if you seek me, you will find me. There is nothing in this world that love cannot heal and redeem. Over time, even the most painful trials and moments of your life, can be healed with love."

I started writing down what He was saying in my journal. I paused and looked up for a moment.

"I can see a broken vessel with cracks and chips all over it. It would seem as if this vessel should be thrown out because it no longer has any value or worth, it's too broken. But you come with gold and you pour it into every crack and it restores the vessel and makes it whole. And it now has more value and beauty than it did before. Also before it was broken I couldn't see it shine the light it carried within, and now it shines the most extraordinary light."

"Now you are seeing with my eyes. Do you remember Joseph's words to his brothers in Genesis when he said, "You meant evil against me, but God intended it for good to accomplish what is now being done, the saving of many lives."

I held onto this thought for a moment and said to Jesus, "Yes I do. And I imagine that day when you went to the cross, darkness was declaring victory. Having taken life from the light of the world and turning your very own against you unto death. Yet, you used that moment to fulfill every word spoken, revealing your faithfulness and glory to the world as you conquered death once and for all. And what seemed like a victory for darkness that day, released the greatest light the world had ever known. Your love. Because even in the face of rejection, you still chose us. How did you survive that pain?"

He stopped for a moment and looked at the sun rising higher and higher above the trees before us. The golden light was illuminating His face as He soaked in the warm rays.

"Everything in this world is temporary, with the exception of one thing. Love." He said this and looked over to me to see how I would respond to His words.

I nodded a little but gave him a 'keep going' face.

"Love is the only driving force in this world that is eternal, all else fades and cannot endure. In other words, you can't take your

167

pain with you into eternity with me. Love and pain do not exist together in Eden. Here, I want to show you."

With that I closed my eyes tightly again, I knew how much Jesus loved to show me things and never bored of the places He liked to take me.

I could still feel the breeze on my face and the warm sunlight the day was releasing over us, but what my eyes were seeing in my imagination was a garden unlike anything I had ever been to before. We walked through tall brush that was green and full of life. Together hand and hand He led me around the garden.

"What do you feel here?"

My face said it all, "I feel peace, love and joy. I don't know that I have ever felt so safe before. Why is that?"

"Because we are in Eden. There is no fear or pain here. Nothing to worry about."

I interrupted, "YES! That is it! I don't know if I remember a time in my life when I wasn't worrying about something or afraid of something."

Jesus laughed loudly, "I do know this about you! You love to think about the worst thing that could happen to you and plan a great deal of your life around avoiding those possibilities."

"I Do!" I agreed through my laughter. "It is almost like a superpower."

We came to a clearing and Jesus held me from moving forward. From where we stood it was like we were back in the moment of creation when Adam was formed from the dust of the earth. We watched as the breath of life flowed into his nostrils.

"This breath can create life. The Word can speak and bring forth anything at any moment. But there is one thing that cannot be created."

I was listening to every word as my eyes were fixed on the scene before us.

"A human heart. For the heart is the seat of the will and choice of creation. Free will has been given to every one of you. For the very essence of love is choice."

My face was hardened as I spoke, "This choice we have been given feels like a curse sometimes and not a blessing. I wish it would be taken away so we didn't screw everything up all the time. Then maybe pain and fear wouldn't have to exist."

Jesus responded, "If that happened, there would be no love. It is the design that you choose to love me. This is the big love story that you speak about so often, don't forget that. Because I will never stop choosing and loving you."

My lips released a familiar scripture from John's Gospel, "In the beginning was the Word, and the Word was with God, and the Word was God. He was in the beginning with God. Through Him all things came into being and not one thing came into being without him. In Him was life and the life was the light of men."

I opened my eyes and looked deeply into His, "Did you know? Did you know here in this moment that Adam and Eve would not obey the command they were given, that they would eat from the wrong tree and choose the wrong voice to listen to. Did you know what would happen next? Surely you didn't. Why would you have created us at all if you had known?"

I didn't stop to wait for Him to answer before I started sharing my next thought, "I can see the life and the light flowing into Adam, but if you knew that over time the world would reject the light, you could have stopped right now. All you would see are hearts turning away from you and each other from this moment on." Pain pierced through me as I thought of the cross again.

"Don't be troubled Jessie. This isn't a story of how darkness conquers light. This is a story of how light shines in the darkness and darkness can never extinguish it."

Eyes opened, I looked up to see birds flying above where we both sat. I picked up my pen and started writing things down. I took as much time as I needed to record all we had just seen together.

Finally I spoke, "If choice is what makes our hearts able to choose love, and you know everything before it happens, doesn't that remove choice in way? Are they really our choices if you have the foresight and knowledge of it all? Then it doesn't even feel like a love story because it's like you are on the outside looking in instead of it unfolding with us in the present."

"My knowledge is different than your knowledge. My knowledge is experienced. It's called out from eternity. It's present in all things that have ever been and are yet to be." He paused and thought for a moment. "How about this, do you want to see one more thing today?"

"Always." I smiled.

"Good answer. Then I would like to take you somewhere you have never been before."

"Oh that sounds marvelous, let's go." I replied while clapping my hands together eagerly.

"But I have to make breakfast for the kids soon and I don't know if we will be able to answer any of my questions today."

Jesus let out a robust laugh at my remark and proceeded to invite me one last time to a place He was eager to show me. I got comfortable in my chair once again and let Him lead the way in the landscape of my mind.

Before I knew it, we were standing side by side in a place that looked like a room with glass ceilings and floors and all around us were star filled skies. The stars danced and glimmered with every color of the rainbow. They almost looked like they were alive in the way they moved.

"Where are we? I asked curiously.

"Look at this." He said as He drew my attention to a moment that I can only explain was outside of time.

The Father was standing up straight and glowing a brilliant golden glow. With one hand He took hold of the light that was emanating from Him and pulled it out of His chest. As He did this the most wonderful thing happened. He placed it into a form that He was knitting together that was before Him. As He did this I saw the detail and the workmanship of His hands. He was creating something magnificent. I watched as He took time with every single moment, every detail, every part of this life that He was creating before Him. Time was nothing to Him here, He had all the time in the world to care for and tend to every detail of this life created in His own Image.

When He was finished I saw the most brilliant life explode before my eyes. He wept with tears of how much this life moved His heart. He was glorified by the work of His hands through the way this light radiated and reflected His glow. He stood in wonder and awe at His perfect creation.

"Psalm 139." Jesus whispered to me.

This jolted me back to the present day and I reached for my purple Bible that was nearby. I opened quickly to the pages to see what they would reveal; "You have searched me and known me. You know my sitting down and my rising up. You understand my thoughts even when I am far away. You know my path. You know when I lie down. You are familiar with all of my ways." I stopped for a minute and closed my eyes again to see the way The Father looked at His creation in the glass room. I grabbed my journal and pen and wrote out a few thoughts and went back to my Bible to read through the rest of the Psalm.

"Where can I go from your Spirit? Where can I flee from your presence? If I go up to the heavens, you are there. If I make my bed in the depths, you are there. If I rise on the wings of the dawn, if I settle on the far side of the sea even there your hand will guide me, your right hand will hold me fast. If I say surely the darkness shall cover me, and night wraps itself around me, even the darkness is not dark to you, the night will shine like the day for darkness is as light to you."

I had no idea prior to this moment what the Psalmist had written on these pages thousands of years ago. But what I was reading were the very thing I had just experienced. He had shown me how there was nowhere I could go without His presence.

Today alone, we had sat in heavenly places, on the wings of the dawn and journeyed from the far side of the sea where He showed me how His hand would always be holding onto mine. He showed me how darkness could never extinguish the light, a knowledge that was too wonderful and great for me, just as the Psalmist expressed. Turning to Jesus I read out loud, "For you created my inmost being, you covered me in my mother's womb. I praise you because I am fearfully and wonderfully made, marvelous are your works that my soul knows very well. My frame was not hidden from you when I was made in the secret place, when I was woven together in the depths of the earth and soil. My unformed being saw your eyes and in your book were written all the days that were formed for me, before one of them came to be. How precious are your thoughts of me. If I tried to count them, then they would outnumber the sand."

"Thank you for this my Lord. I feel like you have given me a gift of seeing this with my own eyes today."

Jesus knew I was still trying to understand something that was far too great for me so He offered these final thoughts.

"I know you are struggling with understanding the plans I have for you and how it all works. One day you will understand more, but at this moment I'm asking you to walk with me."

"Walk with you? That is easier said than done sometimes." There have been times that I have felt you holding onto me, and others as if you threw me out to sea."

"I know it felt that way for you. There was never a single tear you cried in those moments of your life that I didn't see or feel. Your pain is my pain. I'm not able to separate your hurt from my own. The reason you feel it is because you were made in my very own image. You feel pain because you are a child of light and you carry my heart. When darkness touches light you feel its sting. Light exposes darkness for what it is."

"But I thought you said, pain is not eternal." I questioned.

"It isn't." He answered.

"So how is it that you, being eternal, can still feel pain?"

"This is the great mystery of the I AM, but it is the very key to understanding love and presence. It may be hard to comprehend that I have no beginning and no end, I am present in every moment and every living thing. This is how I cannot be separated from your joy or your pain. But I can promise you this, your pains from this life will fade. Do you remember the birth of your children and the way the greatest pain you had felt gave way to the greatest love you had ever known?"

"How could I forget, yet you are right. It is something I only recall as memory. I don't feel that pain anymore. So, if you saw how this story ends from the very beginning, you must have decided that all of this pain was worth it?"

I rested my head on His shoulder and He put His arm around me. "There is no greater thing in all of creation than love. And there is nothing I wouldn't do to make you feel my love."

"So this really is a love story." I said as I closed my prayer journal for the day.

"It is. And there is so much more to come that you have yet to see, hope or imagine."

"Same time tomorrow then?" I said with a sarcastic laugh.

"Didn't I answer all of your questions yet?" He pleaded.

"Not even close. I don't know if we got anywhere today, my Lord. I think I have more questions than I did before we started this conversation." I gave Him a wink as I hugged Him one last time before I went off to start my day.

He watched me vanish and looked up to the sun that was now midday. Laughing to Himself He uttered, "Some stars shine so brightly they burn me out."

"I heard that!" I yelled from inside the screened door.

"I'll have more questions for you tomorrow! And I'll make sure to bring extra coffee this time. We will both need it! "

NOTES

Chapter 1

    1. E. James Wilder, Anna Kang, John Loppnow, Sungshim Loppnow, *Joyful Journey*: *Listening to Immanuel* (Los Angeles, CA: Presence and Practice, 2015), 2.

Chapter 2

    1. Jim Wilder, "Developing Joy Strength - Jim Wilder," *YouTube*, BRMinistries, 13 Oct 2014, https://www.youtube.com/watch?v=_ftJOk_RJS0.

    2. Alan Wright, *The Power to Bless* (Grand Rapids, MI: Baker Books, 2021), 148.

    3. Ibid., 148.

Chapter 5

    1. Matt Beckenham, *Eden's Blueprint* (Jacksonville, FL: Truly loved Media, 2022) 21.

Chapter 7

    1. Dr. James Wilder, "Dr. Jim Wilder Sessions 1-8," *You Tube, Luke 4:18 Ministries*, 26 February 2019. https://www.youtube.com/@Luke418Ministries.

    2. E. James Wilder, Anna Kang, John Loppnow, Sungshim Loppnow, *Joyful Journey*: *Listening to*

Immanuel (Los Angeles, CA: Presence and Practice, 2015), 27.

3. Ibid., 26.

Chapter 8

1. Jen Wilkin, *Women of the Word* (Wheaton, Illinois: Crossway, 2014), 55.

Chapter 9

1. Gene Edwards, *A Tale of Three Kings* (Carol Stream, Illinois: Tyndale House Publishers, Inc.,1980) , 75.
2. James G. Friesen, E. James Wilder, Anne M. Bierling, Rick Koepcke, Maribeth Poole, *Living from the Heart Jesus Gave You* (East Peoria, Illinois: Shepherd's House, Inc. 1999), 102.
3. Gene Edwards, *A Tale of Three Kings*, 24.
4. Dr. Jim Wilder, "Fourth Annual Nurture Conference: Spiritual Formation and the Healing of the Inner Person," 14 May 2022, Lipscomb University, Nashville, TN. Keynote Speaker.

Chapter 10

1. Dr. Jim Wilder, "Satan's First Strategy: Avoiding Pain*"*, *Internet Archive*, September 22, 2014, https://archive.org/details/SatansFirstStategyAvoiding Pain.

Chapter 11

1. Jessie DeCorsey, "Writing Assignment #4 – Final", 12 May 2021, *Book of Job*, Luther Seminary, Student Paper.
2. Matitiahu Tsevat, "The Meaning of the Book of Job," *Hebrew Union College Annual*, vol. 37, 1966, 28. *JSTOR*, http://www.jstor.org/stable/23503115.

3. To Make You Feel My Love, *Garth Brooks*, Hope Floats – Music from the Motion Picture Album, 1998.

Chapter 12

1. Rev. Andrea Joy Holroyd, "What is the difference between transfigured and transformed?" *Blog*, Schoharie Presbyterian, 28 February 2019. https://www.schohariepresbyterian.org/blog/february282019

2. Jim Wilder, *Renovated: God, Dallas Willard & the Church That Transforms* (Colorado Springs, Co: NavPress, 2020), 82.

3. Ibid., 83-84.

4. E. James Wilder, Anna Kang, John Loppnow, Sungshim Loppnow, *Joyful Journey: Listening to Immanuel* (Los Angeles, CA: Presence and Practice, 2015), 9-10.

Chapter 13

1. Jonathan Young, "Community Mourns Longtime Teacher," 2 December 2016, *The Gazette*, Stillwater, Minnesota.

2. Michel Hendricks, Jim Wilder, *The Other Half of Church: Christian Community, Brain Science, and Overcoming Spiritual Stagnation* (Chicago, Illinois: Moody Publishers, 2020), 93-94.

3. Jessie DeCorsey, "Final Paper," 13 May 2021, *Scripture and its Witness*, Luther Seminary, Student Paper.

4. Stant Litore, *Lives of Unforgetting: What We Lose in Translation When We Read the Bible, and a Way of Reading the Bible as a Call to Adventure* (Westmarch Publishing, 2019), 24.

5. Ibid., 26.

6. Ibid., 24.

7. Alan Wright, *The Power to Bless* (Grand Rapids, MI: Baker Books, 2021), 71.

Chapter 14

1. Gene Edwards, *A Tale of Three Kings* (Carol Stream, Illinois: Tyndale House Publishers, Inc., 1980), 42.
2. Michel Hendricks, Jim Wilder, *The Other Half of Church: Christian Community, Brain Science, and Overcoming Spiritual Stagnation* (Chicago, Illinois: Moody Publishers, 2020), 71.
3. E. James Wilder, Anna Kang, John Loppnow, Sungshim Loppnow, *Joyful Journey*: *Listening to Immanuel* (Los Angeles, CA: Presence and Practice, 2015), 34-35. Describes a mutual mind state. For more characteristics of the mutual mind state I recommend "Dr. Jim Wilder – Session 3," *Luke 4:18 Ministries*, 26 February 2019. https://www.youtube.com/watch?v=AJAQ1sTHw8s&t=4257s.
4. Michel Hendricks, Jim Wilder, *The Other Half of Church,* 84-85.
5. Ibid., 97.
6. Ibid., 114.
7. Ibid., 182-183.

Chapter 15

1. Matt Beckenham, *Eden's Blueprint: Gods Plan For Your Life Began with a Design* (Jacksonville, Florida: Truly Loved Media, 2022), 3.
2. Matt Beckenham, *Eden's Blueprint*, XLI.
3. Ellen F. Davis, *Getting Involved With God: Rediscovering the Old Testament* (Cambridge, Ma: Cowley Publications, 2001), 141.
4. Matt Beckenham, *Eden's Blueprint*, 3.

Chapter 16

1. Matt Beckenham, *Eden's Blueprint: Gods Plan For Your Life Began with a Design* (Jacksonville, Florida: Truly Loved Media, 2022), 82.

2. Ben Smart, "40,000 Denominations Worldwide - Christianity Divided?" *The Ben Smart Blog*, thebensmartblog.com /?s=denominations+worldwide, 12 February 2014.

3. Matt Beckenham, *Eden's Blueprint*, 133.

4. E. James Wilder, Anna Kang, John Loppnow, Sungshim Loppnow, *Joyful Journey*: *Listening to Immanuel* (Los Angeles, CA: Presence and Practice, 2015), 17.

5. James G. Friesen, E. James Wilder, Anne M. Bierling, Rick Koepcke, Maribeth Poole, *Living from the Heart Jesus Gave You* (East Peoria, Illinois: Shepherd's House, Inc. 1999), 82-95.

6. Strong's Concordance, *Bible Hub*, 2021 Discovery Bible, https://biblehub.com/greek/5055.htm.

7. Matt Beckenham, *Eden's Blueprint*, 78.

8. David Curwin, "karov, korban and kerev," Blog, Balashon, 29 March 2020, https://www.balashon.com/2020/03/karov-korban-and-kerev.html. Accessed November 18, 2023.

9. Ellen F. Davis, *Getting Involved With God: Rediscovering the Old Testament* (Cambridge, Ma: Cowley Publications, 2001), 122.

10. Dr. Jim Wilder, "Satan's Second Strategy: The Picker", *Internet Archive*, September 22, 2014, https://archive.org/details/SatansSecondStrategyThePicker.

11. Strong's Concordance, *Bible Hub*, 2021 Discovery Bible, https://biblehub.com/greek/1781.htm.

12. Douglas Harper, "Etymology of Identity," *Online Etymology Dictionary*,

https://www.etymonline.com/word/identity, Accessed
November 19, 2023.

For more paintings in this collection please visit: www.jessiedecorsey.com

Walk With Me painting series by ©Jessie DeCorsey 2023

Walk With Me painting series by ©Jessie DeCorsey 2023

Walk With Me painting series by ©Jessie DeCorsey 2023